T5-CVE-781

Study Guide for use with

FUNDAMENTAL
Accounting Principles

ELEVENTH CANADIAN EDITION

Volume
1

Kermit D. Larson
University of Texas – Austin

Tilly Jensen
Northern Alberta Institute of Technology

Prepared by
K. Suzanne Coombs
Kwantlen University College

McGraw-Hill
Ryerson

Toronto   Montréal   Boston   Burr Ridge, IL   Dubuque, IA   Madison, WI   New York
San Francisco   St. Louis   Bangkok   Bogotá   Caracas   Kuala Lumpur   Lisbon
London   Madrid   Mexico City   Milan   New Delhi   Santiago   Seoul   Singapore
Sydney   Taipei

The McGraw-Hill Companies

McGraw-Hill
Ryerson

Study Guide for use with
Fundamental Accounting Principles
Volume 1
Eleventh Canadian Edition

ISBN: 0-07-091960-7

1 2 3 4 5 6 7 8 9 10 CP 0 9 8 7 6 5

Printed and bound in Canada

Care has been taken to trace ownership of copyright material contained in this text; however, the publisher will welcome any information that enables them to rectify any reference or credit for subsequent editions.

Executive Sponsoring Editor: Nicole Lukach
Marketing Manager: Kim Verhaeghe
Developmental Editor: Brook Nymark
Senior Production Coordinator: Madeleine Harrington
Cover Design: Dianna Little
Printer: Canadian Printco

Contents

CHAPTER 1
ACCOUNTING: THE KEY TO SUCCESS

Learning Objective 1:

Describe accounting and its goals and uses.

Summary

Accounting is an information and measurement system that aims to identify, measure, record and communicate relevant, reliable, consistent, and comparable information about economic activities. It helps us better assess opportunities, products, investments, and social and community responsibilities. The power of accounting is in opening our eyes to new and exciting opportunities. The greatest benefits from understanding accounting often come to those outside of accounting, because an improved understanding of accounting helps us to compete better in today's globally and technologically challenging world.

Learning Objective 2:

Describe forms of business organization.

Summary

Organizations can be classified as either businesses or non-businesses. Businesses are organized for profit, while non-businesses serve us in ways not always measured by profit. Businesses take one of three forms: sole proprietorship, partnership or corporation. These forms of organization have characteristics that hold important implications for legal liability, taxation, continuity, number of owners, and legal status.

Learning Objective 3:

Identify users and uses of accounting.

Summary

There are both internal and external users of accounting. Some users and uses of accounting include: (a) management for control, monitoring and planning; (b) lenders for making decisions regarding loan applications; (c) shareholders for making investment decisions; (d) directors for overseeing management; and (e) employees for judging employment opportunities.

Learning Objective 4:

Explain why ethics and social responsibility are crucial to accounting.

Summary

The goal of accounting is to provide useful information for decision making. For information to be useful, it must be trusted. This demands ethics and socially responsible behaviour in accounting. Without these, accounting information loses its reliability.

Learning Objective 5:

Describe how technology is changing accounting.

Summary

Technology has increased the access to, and processing speed and quantity of, accounting information. Accountants have had to enhance their information technology knowledge and experience in order to compete. However, accountants who possess strong information technology skills are in high market demand and, as a result, earn large salaries.

Learning Objective 6:

Identify opportunities in accounting and related fields.

Summary

Opportunities in accounting and related fields are numerous. They encompass traditional financial and managerial accounting, and taxation, but also include accounting-related fields such as lending, consulting, managing and planning.

Learning Objective 7:

Describe the codes of ethics and professional conduct for accountants.

Summary

Each of the three professional accounting bodies in Canada has a code of professional conduct outlining the ethical standards required of accountants. Failure to comply leads to disciplinary action.

Chapter Outline

I. Accounting goals and uses

A. Power of Accounting

Accounting is an information system that identifies, measures, records and communicates relevant, reliable, consistent and comparable information about an organization's economic activities.

B. Focus of Accounting

The major objective of accounting is to help people make better decisions. *Recordkeeping*, or *bookkeeping*, is the recording of financial transactions and events. Accounting involves recordkeeping, or bookkeeping, but is much more. Accounting also involves designing information systems to provide useful reports to monitor and control and organizations' activities.

II. Forms of Organization

A. Business Organizations

There are three forms of business organization and each form has implications to legal entity, limited liability, unlimited life, business taxes, and number of owners. The three forms are:

1. A *Sole (or Single) Proprietorship* is a business owned by one person. It is not a separate legal entity from its owner. The owner has *unlimited liability*; thus is responsible for debts that are greater than the resources of the proprietorship. Because tax authorities do not separate a proprietorship from its owner, the profits of the business are reported and taxed on the owner's personal income tax return.

2. A *Partnership* is a business owned by two or more persons, called partners, who are subject to unlimited liability. Because the business is not legally separate from its owners, each partner's share of profits is reported and taxed on that partner's tax return. A limited partnership includes a general partner with unlimited liability and a limited partner with limited liability.

3. A *Corporation* is a business that is a separate legal entity whose owners are called shareholders. These owners own shares and have limited liability. A shareholder can sell or transfer shares to another person without affecting the operations of a corporation. A corporation files a tax return and pays tax on its profits.

B. Non-business organizations plan and operate for goals other than profit. They do not have an identifiable owner.

III. Users and Uses of Accounting Information
  A. External information users are not directly involved in running the organization.
    1. External users – lenders, directors, customers, suppliers, regulators, lawyers, brokers, and the press.
    2. External reports called financial statements help users analyze an organization's activities. Generally Accepted Accounting Principles (GAAP) increase the usefulness of financial statements to users.
  B. Internal information users are directly involved in managing and operating an organization.
    1. Managerial accounting is aimed at serving the decision-making needs of internal users. Special purpose reports are customized to meet the information needs of internal users.
    2. Internal operating functions rely on accounting information to ensure the smooth operation of each function.
    3. Internal controls are procedures set up to protect assets, ensure reliable accounting reports, promote efficiency, and ensure that company policies are followed.

IV. Ethics and Social Responsibility
  A. Understanding Ethics—Ethics are beliefs that differentiate right from wrong.
    1. Ethical behaviour is important to the accounting profession and to those who use accounting information.
    2. A lack of ethics makes it more difficult for people to trust one another.
    3. Accountants have ethical obligations: to maintain professional competence, treat sensitive information as confidential, exercise personal integrity, and be objective in matters of financial disclosure.
  B. Organizational Ethics—are likely learned through management example and leadership.
  C. Accounting Ethics—are crucial.
    1. Misleading information can lead to incorrect decisions, causing harm to workers, customers and suppliers.
    2. Codes of ethics for accountants are set up and enforced by the provincial offices of all of the professional accounting bodies.
  D. Social Responsibility—is a concern for the impact of our actions on society as a whole. Organizations are concerned with their social responsibility.

Chapter Outline

Notes

V. Technology: Creating Change in Accounting—technology allows instant access to services, data, news and information to aid business operations

1. Technology allows instant access to services, data, news and information to aid business operations

2. Demands on the accounting profession and businesspeople in general have expanded. Spreadsheet and accounting software application skills are now essential. The need for information technology knowledge and experience is growing.

VI. Accounting Opportunities

A. Accountants work in four broad fields:

1. *Financial Accounting* serves the needs of external users by providing financial statements. An audit is an independent review and test of an organization's accounting systems and record. External auditors perform the audit function.

2. *Managerial Accounting* serves the needs of internal users by providing special purpose reports in areas such as:

   a. General Accounting

   b. Cost Accounting

   c. Budgeting

   d. Internal Auditing

   e. Management Consulting

3. In *Taxation,* tax accountants help taxpayers comply with tax laws by preparing returns and providing tax-planning assistance.

4. *Accounting-Related* opportunities include lending, consulting, managing, planning and other roles.

B. Private accountants work for a single employer. Public accountants provide services to many different clients. Government accountants work for local, provincial, and federal government agencies.

C. Professional Certification—In Canada, several accounting organizations provide the education and training required to obtain professional certification. The three professional accounting designations are:

1. Chartered Accountant (CA)

2. Certified General Accountant (CGA)

3. Certified Management Accountant (CMA)

VII. Appendix 1A—Codes of Ethics and Professional Conduct

A. Certified General Accountants of Alberta

B. Society of Management Accountants of Alberta

C. Institute of Chartered Accountants of Ontario

© McGraw-Hill Ryerson, Inc., 2005

Study Guide, Chapter 1

1-5

Problem I

Many of the important ideas and concepts discussed in Chapter 1 are reflected in the following list of key terms. Test your understanding of these terms by matching the appropriate definitions with the terms. Record the number identifying the most appropriate definition in the blank space next to each term.

7	Accounting		General accounting
	Audit	9	Government accountants
	Bookkeeping		Internal auditors/auditing
2	Budgeting	3	Internal controls
	Business		Internal users
	Business entity principle		Limited liability
	CA		Limited liability partnership
	CCRA		Limited partnership
	CGA		Management consulting
8	CMA	1	Managerial accounting
	Codes of professional conduct		Partnership
	Common shares		Private accountants
	Controller		Public accountants
6	Corporation		Recordkeeping
	Cost accounting		Shareholders
	Costs		Shares
	Ethics		Single proprietorship
	External auditors/auditing	4	Social responsibility
	External users		Sole proprietorship
	Financial accounting		Taxation
	Generally Accepted Accounting Principles (GAAP)	5	Unlimited liability

 1. The area of accounting aimed at serving the decision-making needs of internal users.

2. The process of developing formal plans for future activities, which often serve as a basis for evaluating actual performance.

3. Procedures set up to protect assets, ensure reliable accounting reports, promote efficiency, and encourage adherence to company policies.

4. A commitment to considering the impact and being accountable for the effects that actions might have on society.

5. When the debts of a sole proprietorship or partnerships are greater than its resources, the owner(s) is (are) financially responsible.

6. A business that is a separate legal entity under provincial or federal laws with owners who are called shareholders.

7. An information system that identifies, measures, records and communicates relevant, reliable, consistent, and comparable information about an organization's economic activities.

8. Certified Management Accountant; an accountant who has met the examination, education, and experience requirements of the Society of Management Accountants for an individual professionally competent in accounting.

9. Accountants who work for local, provincial, and federal government agencies.

10. Activities in which suggestions are offered for improving a company's procedures; the suggestions may concern new accounting and internal control systems, new computer systems, budgeting, and employee benefit plans.

11. Accountants who provide their services to many different clients.

12. Chartered Accountant; an accountant who has met the examination, education, and experience requirements of the Institute of Chartered Accountants for an individual professionally competent in accounting.

13. Persons using accounting information who are not directly involved in the running of the organization. Examples include shareholders, customers, regulators, and suppliers.

14. Sets of guidelines governing the behaviour of the professional.

15. The expenses incurred to earn revenues.

16. Includes both general partner(s) with unlimited liability and limited partner(s) with liability restricted to the amount invested.

17. Persons using accounting information who are directly involved in managing and operating an organization; examples include managers and officers.

18. The owners of a corporation.

19. A check of an organization's accounting systems and records.

20. Accountants work for a single employer other than the government or a public accounting firm.

21. Certified General Accountant; an accountant who has met the examination, education, and experience requirements of the Certified General Accountants' Association for an individual professionally competent in accounting.

22. The field of accounting that includes preparing tax returns and planning future transactions to minimize the amount of tax paid; involves private, public, and government accountants.

23. Canada Customs and Revenue Agency; the federal government agency responsible for the collection of tax and enforcement of tax laws.

24. A business owned by two or more people, which is not organized as a corporation.

25. Restricts partners' liabilities to their own acts and the acts of individuals under their control.

26. The chief accounting officer of an organization.

27. The rules that indicate acceptable accounting practice.

28. A business owned by one person, which is not organized as a corporation; also called a single proprietorship.

29. The part of accounting that involves recording economic transactions and events, either electronically or manually; also called recordkeeping.

30. Employees within organizations who assess whether managers are following established operating procedures and evaluate the efficiency of operating procedures.

31. Examine and provide assurance that financial statements are prepared according to generally accepted accounting principles (GAAP).

32. A business owned by one individual, which is not organized as a corporation; also called a sole proprietorship.

© McGraw-Hill Ryerson, Inc., 2005

33. One or more individuals selling products or services for profit.

34. The name for a corporation's shares when only one class of share capital is issued.

35. The owner's liability is limited to the amount of investment in the business.

36. The recording of financial transactions and events, either manually or electronically; also called bookkeeping.

37. A managerial accounting activity designed to help managers identify, measure, and control operating costs.

38. The task of recording transactions, processing data, and preparing reports for managers; includes preparing financial statements for disclosure to external users.

39. Every business is accounted for separately from its owner's personal activities.

40. Units of ownership in a corporation.

41. Beliefs that differentiate right from wrong.

42. The area of accounting aimed at serving external users.

Solutions for Chapter 1

Problem I

7	Accounting	38	General accounting
19	Audit	9	Government accountants
29	Bookkeeping	30	Internal auditors/auditing
2	Budgeting	3	Internal controls
33	Business	17	Internal users
39	Business entity principle	35	Limited liability
12	CA	25	Limited liability partnership
23	CCRA	16	Limited partnership
21	CGA	10	Management consulting
8	CMA	1	Managerial accounting
14	Codes of professional conduct	24	Partnership
34	Common shares	20	Private accountants
26	Controller	11	Public accountants
6	Corporation	36	Recordkeeping
37	Cost accounting	18	Shareholders
15	Costs	40	Shares
41	Ethics	32	Single proprietorship
31	External auditors/auditing	4	Social responsibility
13	External users	28	Sole proprietorship
42	Financial accounting	22	Taxation
27	Generally Accepted Accounting Principles (GAAP)	5	Unlimited liability

Learning Objective 1:

Identify and explain the content and reporting aims of financial statements.

Summary

The major financial statements are: income statement (shows a company's profitability determined as revenues less expenses equals net income or loss), statement of owner's equity (explains how owner's equity changes from the beginning to the end of a period), balance sheet (reports on a company's financial position, including asset6s, liabilities, and owner's equity), and cash flow statement (identifying all cash inflows and outflows for the period). The differences in financial statements across forms of business organization are: 1. The name of the equity section of the balance sheet: owner's equity for a sole proprietorship, partners' equity for a partnership, and shareholders' equity for a corporation; 2. Distributions of assets to the owner(s) are called withdrawals for both a sole proprietorship and partnership, and dividends for a corporation; 3. When the owner of a proprietorship or partnership is its manager, no salary expense is reported, while in a corporation, salaries paid to managers who are also shareholders are reported as expenses.

Learning Objective 2:

Identify, explain and apply accounting principles.

Summary

Accounting principles aid in producing relevant, reliable, consistent, and comparable information. The general principles described in this chapter include: business entity, cost, objectivity, going concern, monetary unit, and revenue recognition. We will discuss others in later chapters. The business entity principle means that a business is accounted for separately from its owner. The cost principle means financial statements are based on actual costs incurred in business transactions. The objectivity principle means information is supported by independent, objective evidence. He going concern principle means financial statements reflect an assumption that the business continues to operate. The monetary unit principle assumes that transactions can be captured in money terms and that the monetary unit is stable over time. The revenue recognition principle means revenue is recognized when earned, assets received from selling products and services do not have to be in cash, and revenue recognized is measured by cash received plus the cash equivalent (market) value of other assets received.

Learning Objective 3:

Explain and interpret the accounting equation.

Summary

Investing activities are funded by an organization's financing activities. An organization's assets (investments) must equal its financing (from liabilities and from equity). This basic relation gives us the accounting equation: Assets = Liabilities + Owner's Equity.

Learning Objective 4:

Analyze business transactions using the accounting equation.

Summary

A transaction is an exchange of economic consideration between two parties and affects the accounting equation. The equation is always in balance when business transactions are properly recorded. An economic consideration is something of value; examples include products, services, money and rights to collect money. Source documents are the source of accounting information. An event does not involve an economic exchange; it has no effect on the accounting equation.

Learning Objective 5:

Prepare financial statements from business transactions.

Summary

Using the accounting equation, business transactions can be summarized and organized so we can readily prepare the financial statements. The balance sheet uses the ending balances in the accounting equation at a point in time. The statement of owner's equity and the income statement use data from the owner's equity account for the period.

Learning Objective 6: (Appendix 2A)

Describe the process by which generally accepted accounting principles are established.

Summary

Specific accounting principles for financial accounting are established in Canada by the Accounting Standards Board (AcSB), with input from various contributing bodies. Auditing standards are established by the Auditing Standards Board (ASB). The International Accounting Standards Committee (IASC) identifies preferred practices and encourages their adoption throughout the world.

Chapter Outline

I. **Communicating Through Financial Statements**

Organizations report their accounting information to internal and external users in the form of financial statements. Statements reveal an organization's financial health and performance.

A. Previewing Financial Statements

There are four major financial statements: income statement, balance sheet, statement of owner's equity, and cash flow statement. The statements are linked in time in that a balance sheet reports on an organization's financial position at a *point in time*, whereas the income statement, statement of owner's equity, and cash flow statement report on performance over a *period of time,* resulting in a new balance sheet at the end of the period. A one-year reporting period, known as the accounting or fiscal year, is common.

1. *The income statement* reports revenues earned less expenses incurred by a business over a period of time.

    a. *Revenues*— values of assets exchanged for products and services provided to customers as part of the business's main operations.

    b. *Expenses*—costs incurred or the using up of assets from generating revenues. *Assets* are economic resources held by a business and include cash, equipment, buildings, and land.

    c. Net income (profit) — revenues are more than expenses; or net loss— expenses are more than revenues.

2. *The statement of owner's equity* reports on changes in equity over the reporting period. The statement starts with beginning equity and adjusts it.

    a. Increases occur with investments by the owner and/or net income.

    b. Decreases occur with withdrawals by the owner and/or a net loss.

3. *The balance sheet, or statement of financial position,* reports the financial position of the business at a point in time, usually at the end of a month or year, by listing the dollar amount of the assets, liabilities and equity. Total assets equals total liabilities plus equity.

    a. *Assets*—properties or economic resources owned by the business. Assets provide future benefits to the company.

    b. *Liabilities*—debts or obligations of a business; claims of others against assets. Liabilities reduce future assets or require future services or products.

     c. *Equity*—the owner's claim on the assets or the assets that remain after deducting liabilities; also called *net assets*.

  4. *The cash flow statement* describes the sources and uses of cash for a reporting period. The cash flow statement is organized by operating, investing, and financing activities. The statement also reports the beginning, ending and change in cash.

B. Financial Statements and Forms of Organizations

  1. The equity section on the balance sheet is called owner's equity for a sole proprietorship, partners' equity for a partnership, and shareholders' equity for a corporation.

  2. Distributions to owners are called withdrawals in a sole proprietorship, withdrawals in a partnership, and dividends in a corporation.

  3. When managers are also owners, their salaries are not an expense in a sole proprietorship, not an expense in a partnership, and an expense in a corporation.

II. Generally Accepted Accounting Principles (GAAP)

A. Setting accounting principles

The responsibility for setting accounting principles is determined by individuals and groups as discussed in Appendix 2A. A primary purpose of GAAP is to make information in financial statements relevant, reliable, consistent, and comparable.

B. Fundamental Principles of Accounting
General principles that make up acceptable accounting practices:

  1. *Business entity principle*—each economic entity or business of the owner must keep accounting records and reports that are separate from those of the owner and any other economic entity of the owner.

  2. *Cost principle*—all transactions are recorded based on the actual cash amount received or paid. The cash or cash-equivalent amount of the exchange is recorded.

  3. *Objectivity principle*—financial statement information must be supported by independent, unbiased, and verifiable evidence.

  4. *Going-concern principle*—financial statements users assume that the statements reflect a business that is going to continue its operations instead of being closed or sold.

5. *Monetary unit principle*—transactions are expressed using units of money as the common denominator. It is assumed that the monetary unit is stable therefore a transaction is left as originally recorded and is not later adjusted for changes in currency value or inflation.

6. *Revenue recognition principle*—revenue is recorded at the time it is earned regardless of whether cash or another asset has been exchanged. The amount of revenue to be recorded is measured by the cash plus the cash equivalent (market) value of any other assets received.

III. Transactions and the Accounting Equation

A. The *accounting equation* (*balance sheet equation*) describes the relationship between a company's assets, liabilities, and equity. It is expressed as:

Assets = Liabilities   + Owner's Equity.

Or: Assets = Non-Owner Financing + Owner Financing

Net Assets = Assets - Liabilities

IV.   **Transaction analysis**—A business transaction is an exchange of economic consideration between two parties that causes a change in the assets, liabilities, or owner's equity. An economic consideration is something of value. Every transaction leaves the equation in balance.

1. Investment by owner =
    +Asset (Cash) = + Owner's Equity (Owner's Name, Capital)

2. Purchase supplies for cash =
    +Asset (Supplies) = −Asset (Cash)
    Increase and decrease on the asset side of the equation keeps the equation in balance.

3. Purchase furniture and supplies on credit =
    +Asset (Supplies) +Asset (Furniture) = + Liability (Accounts Payable)
    Increases on both sides of equation keeps equation in balance.

4. Services rendered for cash =
    + Asset (Cash) = + Owner's Equity (Owner's Name, Capital)
    Reason: revenue earned
    Increase on both sides of equation keeps equation in balance.

5. & 6. Payment of expenses in cash =
    − Asset (Cash) = − Owner's Equity (Owner's Name, Capital)
    Reason: expenses (rent, salaries) incurred.
    Decrease on both sides of equation keeps equation in balance.

7. Service contract signed for future periods
    No effect to assets, liabilities, or owner's equity
    Reason: no economic exchange.

8. Services and rental revenues rendered for credit =
    + Asset (Accounts Receivable) = + Owner's Equity (Owner's Name, Capital)
    Reason: revenue earned
    Increase on both sides of equation keeps equation in balance.

9. Receipt of cash on account =
    + Asset (Cash) = − Asset (Accounts Receivable)
    Increase and decrease on one side of the equation keeps equation in balance.

10. Payment of an accounts payable =
    − Asset (Cash) = − Liability (Accounts Payable)
    Decrease on both sides of equation keeps equation in balance.

11. Withdrawal of cash by owner =
    − Asset (Cash) = − OE (Owner's Name, Capital)
    Decrease on both sides of equation keeps equation in balance.

V. Financial Statements

Financial statements are prepared from business transactions.

A. Income Statement—revenues and expense information is taken from the owner's equity column. Revenues are reported first, expenses follow, and net income (loss) is reported at the bottom and is the amount earned during the period.

B. Statement Owner's Equity—the beginning balance of owner's equity is the balance as of the end of the prior reporting period. Investments of the owner during the period are added. The net income from the income statement is added (or the net loss is subtracted) and the owner's withdrawals for the period are subtracted to arrive at the ending capital.

C. Balance Sheet—the amounts appearing on the balance sheet are the ending balance of each asset, liability, and owner's equity. The left side of the balance sheet lists assets. The right side lists liabilities and owner's equity. The owner's equity balance is the ending balance from the statement of owner's equity. The total of liabilities plus owner's equity must equal total assets to prove the accounting equation.

VI. Developing Accounting Standards—(Appendix 2A)

A. Generally Accepted Accounting Principles (GAAP)—are identified in response to the needs of users and others affected by financial accounting, and are developed primarily by the Accounting Standards Board (AcSB). Audits are performed in accordance with Generally Accepted Auditing Standards (GAAS) that are developed by the Auditing Standards Board (ASB). Finalized recommendations from these bodies are published as part of the CICA Handbook, having the force of law under the Canada Business Corporations Act.

B. International Accounting Standards—are addressed by the International Accounting Standards Committee (IASC), by identifying preferred accounting practices and then encouraging their worldwide acceptance.

BASIC ACCOUNTING EQUATION

ASSETS = LIABILITIES + OWNER'S EQUITY

Warning: No matter what happens always keep this scale in balance

TRANSACTION ANALYSIS RULES

1) Every transaction affects at least two items.

2) Every transaction must result in a balanced equation.

TRANSACTION ANALYSIS POSSIBILITIES:

A		=	L + OE
(1) +		And	+
Or (2) -		And	-
Or (3) + and -		And	No change
Or (4) No change		And	+ and -

Problem I

The following statements are either true or false. Place a (T) in the parentheses before each true statement and an (F) before each false statement.

1. ( ) Equipment appraised at $12,000 and worth that much to its purchaser should be recorded at its worth ($12,000), even though it was purchased on sale for $10,000.

2. ( ) The owner of a business must keep accounting records for the business separate from personal records.

3. ( ) The statement of financial position shows a company's revenues, expenses, and net income or loss.

4. ( ) Owner investments + Net income − Owner withdrawals = The increase in liabilities during the year.

5. ( ) Revenue is recorded at the time it is earned regardless of whether cash or another asset has been exchanged.

Problem II

You are given several words, phrases, or numbers to choose from in completing each of the following statements or in answering the following questions. In each case select the one that best completes the statement, or answers the question, and place its letter in the answer space provided.

_____ 1. Financial statement information about Boom Company is as follows:

December 31, 2005:

    Assets $27,000

    Liabilities 20,000

December 31, 2006:

    Assets..30,000

    Liabilities...13,600

During 2006:

    Net income..14,000

    Owner investments...?

    Owner withdrawals 16,000

The amount of owner investments during 2006 is:

a. $2,000.

b. $11,400.

c. $14,000.

d. $0.

e. Some other amount.

_____ 2.   The authoritative committee that identifies generally accepted auditing standards is the:

   a.   OSC.

   b.   AcSB.

   c.   FEI

   d.   ASB

   e.   CICA

_____ 3.   The objectivity principle:

   a.   Provides guidance on when revenue should be reflected on the income statement; revenue should be recognized at the time it is earned; allows the inflow of assets associated with revenue may be in a form other than cash, and the amount of revenue should be measured as the cash plus the cash equivalent value of any noncash assets received from customers in exchange for goods or services.

   b.   Requires financial statements to reflect the assumption that the business will continue operating instead of being closed or sold, unless evidence shows that it will not continue.

   c.   Requires that every business be accounted for separately from its owner or owners.

   d.   Requires that financial statement information be supported by unbiased evidence, rather than someone's opinion.

   e.   Requires that financial statements be based on actual costs incurred in business transactions; where cost is cash or cash-equivalent amount given in exchange.

_____ 4.   Obligations of a business or organization or claims against assets, are called:

   a.   Assets.

   b.   Liabilities

   c.   Expenses.

   d.   Revenues.

   e.   Owner's equity.

_____ 5.   Of the four major financial statements, three of the statements report on transactions over a period of time, and one statement reports on an organization's financial position at a point in time. The statement reporting on the financial position at a point in time is the:

   a.   Income statement.

   b.   Statement of owner's equity.

   c.   Cash flow statement.

   d.   Statement of assets.

   e.   Balance sheet.

Problem III

Many of the important ideas and concepts discussed in Chapter 2 are reflected in the following list of key terms. Test your understanding of these terms by matching the appropriate definitions with the terms. Record the number identifying the most appropriate definition in the blank space next to each term.

	Accounting equation		GAAS
	Accounts payable		Generally Accepted Accounting Principles
	Accounts receivable		Generally Accepted Auditing Standards
	AcSB		Going concern principle
	ASB		IASC
	Assets		Income statement
	Balance sheet		Liabilities
	Balance sheet equation		Monetary unit principle
	Business activities		Natural business year
	Business entity principle		Net assets
	Business events		Net income
	Business transaction		Net loss
	Calendar year		Note payable
	Cash flow statement		Objectivity principle
	CICA Handbook		Owner investments
	Comparability		Owner's equity
	Consistency		Owner withdrawals
	Cost principle		Profit
	Creditors		Relevance
	Debtors		Reliability
	Economic consideration		Revenue recognition principle
	Equity		Revenues
	Expenses		Source documents
	Event		Statement of owner's equity
	Financial statements		Statement of financial position
	Fiscal year		Transaction
	GAAP		Withdrawal

1. Similarity; ability to be compared with other information.

2. The excess of expenses over revenues for a period.

3. International Accounting Standards Committee; a committee that attempts to create more harmony among the accounting practices of different countries by identifying preferred practices and encouraging their worldwide acceptance.

4. Accounting Standards Board: the authoritative committee that identifies generally accepted accounting standards.

5. Another name for net income.

6. The principle that requires every business to be accounted for separately from its owner or owners; based on the goal of providing relevant information about each business to users.

7. The distribution of cash or other assets from a proprietorship or partnership to its owner or owners.

8. Costs incurred or the using up of assets as a result of the major or central operations of a business.

9. A liability expressed by a written promise to make a future payment at a specific time.

10. Generally Accepted Accounting Principles

11. The rules adopted by the accounting profession as guides for conducting audits of financial statements.

12. A financial statement that reports the financial position of a business at a point in time; lists the types and dollar amounts of assets, liabilities, and equity as of a specific date; also called the *statement of financial position*.

13. A 12-month period that ends when a company's sales activities are at their lowest point.

14. Generally Accepted Auditing Standards

15. An accounting year that begins January 1 and ends December 31.

16. A description of the relationship between a company's asset, liabilities, and equity; expressed as Assets = Liabilities + Owner's Equity; also called the *balance sheet equation*.

17. The transfer of an owner's personal assets to their business.

18. Provides guidance on when revenue should be reflected on the income statement; the rule states that revenue is recorded at the time it is earned regardless of whether cash or another asset has been exchanged.

19. Individuals or organizations entitled to receive payments from a company.

20. A financial statement that reports the changes in equity over the reporting period; beginning equity is adjusted for increases such as owner investment or net income and for decreases such as owner withdrawals or a net loss.

21. Activities that do not involve an exchange of economic consideration between two parties and therefore do not affect the accounting equation.

22. A one-year reporting period.

23. Information must make a difference in the decision-making process.

24. Another name for business transaction.

25. A financial statement that describes the sources and uses of cash for a reporting period, i.e., where a company's cash came from (receipts) and where it went during the period (payments); the cash flows are arranged by an organization's major activities: operating, investing, and financing activities.

26. An asset created by selling products or services on credit.

27. The financial statement that shows, by subtracting expenses from revenues, whether the business earned a profit; it lists the types and amounts of revenues earned and expenses incurred by a business over a period of time.

28. Conformity with other or earlier information; using the same accounting procedures from one accounting period to the next.

29. Assets minus liabilities; another name for equity.

30. A business event.

31. Something of value (e.g., products, services, money, and rights to collect money).

32. The publication of the Canadian Institute for Chartered Accountants that details generally accepted accounting principles in Canada.

33. The accounting guideline that requires financial statement information to be supported by independent, unbiased evidence rather than someone's opinion; adds to the reliability, verifiability, and usefulness of accounting information.

34. Documents that identify and describe transactions entering the accounting process; the source of accounting information, whether in paper or electronic form.

35. Individuals or organizations that owe amounts to a business.

36. Auditing Standards Board: the authoritative committee that identifies generally accepted auditing standards.

37. The expression of transactions and events in money units; examples include units such as the Canadian dollar, American dollar, peso, and pound sterling.

38. The rule that requires financial statements to reflect the assumption that the business will continue operating instead of being closed or sold, unless evidence shows that it will not continue.

39. Another name for the accounting equation.

40. Total assets minus total liabilities; represents how much of the assets belong to the owner. Increases with owner investments and net income and decreases with owner withdrawals and net loss.

41. All of the transactions and events experienced by a business.

42. The excess of revenues over expenses for a period.

43. Another name for the balance sheet.

44. An exchange of economic consideration between two parties that causes a change in assets, liabilities, or owner's equity. Examples of economic considerations include products, services, money, and rights to collect money.

45. Another name for withdrawals.

46. The value of assets exchanged for goods or services provided to customers as part of the business's main operations; may occur as inflows of assets or decreases in liabilities.

47. The most important products of accounting; include the balance sheet, income statement, statement of owner's equity, and cash flow statement.

48. The owner's claim on the assets of a business; more precisely, the assets of an entity that remain after deducting its liabilities; also called *net assets*.

49. The debts or obligations of a business; claims by others that will reduce the future assets of a business or require future services or products.

50. The accounting principle that requires financial statement information to be based on actual costs incurred in business transactions; it requires assets and services to be recorded initially at the cash or cash equivalent amount given in exchange.

51. Properties or economic resources owned by the business; more precisely, resources with an ability to provide future benefits to the business.

52. A liability created by buying goods or services on credit.

53. The extent to which information is verifiable and neutral; implies a consensus among different measures.

54. The rules adopted by the accounting profession that make up acceptable accounting practices for the preparation of financial statements.

Problem IV

Complete the following by filling in the blanks.

1. Expenses are outflows or the _____ of assets as a result of the major or central operations of a business.

2. Assets created by selling goods and services on credit are called _____. Liabilities created by buying goods and services on credit are called _____.

3. The balance sheet equation is _____ equals _____ plus _____. It is also called the _____ equation.

4. An excess of revenues over expenses for a period results in a _____. An excess of expenses over revenues results in a _____. The financial statement that lists revenues and expenses is the _____.

5. A balance sheet prepared for a business shows its financial position as of a specific _____. Financial position is shown by listing the _____ of the business, its _____, and its _____.

6. Equity on a balance sheet is the difference between a company's _____ and its _____.

7. Probable future sacrifices of economic benefits arising from present obligations of a particular entity to transfer assets or provide services to other entities in the future as a result of past transactions or events are called _____.

8. Individuals or organizations entitled to receive payment from a company are called _____ and those owing money to a business are called _____.

9. Under the _____ principle every business is to be accounted for as a separate entity separate and distinct from its _____ or _____.

10. The cash flow statement shows the events that caused _____ to change. It classifies the cash flow into three major categories: _____, _____, and _____ activities.

11. The statement of owner's equity discloses all changes in equity during the period including _____, _____, and _____.

12. The cost principle requires financial statement information to be based on _____ incurred in business transactions. The going-concern principle requires financial statements to reflect the assumption that the business will _____ instead of being _____ or _____. The revenue recognition principle requires that revenue be recognized at the time it is _____.

Problem V

The assets, liabilities, and owner's equity of Jody Leung's consulting business are shown on the first line in the equation below, and following the equation are eight transactions completed by Ms. Leung. Show by additions and subtractions in the spaces provided the effects of each transaction on the items of the equation. Show new totals after each transaction as in Illustration 2-14 in the text.

		Assets			= Liabilities +	Owner's Equity
Cash	Accounts + Receivable +	Prepaid Rent	+ Supplies	+ Office Equipment =	Accounts Payable +	J. Leung, Capital
$7,000			$1,000	$12,000		$20,000

1. _____

2. _____

3. _____

4. _____

5. _____

6. _____

7. _____

8. _____

9. _____

1. Paid the rent for four months in advance on the business office, $4,000.
2. Paid cash to purchase supplies for the office, $750.
3. Completed consulting work for Albert Finney and immediately collected the full payment of $1,800 in cash.
4. Purchased office equipment on credit, $1,500.
5. Completed $1,600 of computer work for Roy Rouge and billed the client.
6. Paid for the computer equipment purchased in Transaction 4.
7. Received $1,600 from Roy Rouge for the consulting work in Transaction 5.
8. Paid the weekly salary of the assistant, $800.
9. Jody Leung withdrew $1,300 cash from the business for personal expenses.

Refer to your completed equation and fill in the blanks:

a. Did each transaction affect two items of the equation? _____

b. Did the equation remain in balance after the effects of each transaction were entered? _____

c. If the equation had not remained in balance after the effects of each transaction were entered, this would have indicated that _____.

d. Ms. Leung earned $1,800 of revenue upon the completion of Transaction 3, and the asset that flowed into the business as a result of this transaction was in the form of _____.

e. Ms. Leung earned $1,600 of revenue upon the completion of Transaction 5, and the asset that flowed into the business upon the completion of this transaction was _____.

f. The right to collect $1,600 from Roy Rouge was converted into _____ in Transaction 7. Nevertheless, the revenue was earned upon the completion of the _____ in Transaction 5.

g. The $1,600 collected in Transaction 7 was recognized as revenue in Transaction 5 because of the _____ principle, which states that (1) revenue should be recognized at the time it is _____; (2) the inflow of assets associated with revenue may be in a form other than _____; and (3) the amount of revenue should be measured as the cash plus the cash equivalent value of any _____ received from customers in exchange for goods or services.

Solutions for Chapter 2

Problem I

1. F
2. T
3. F
4. F
5. T

Problem II

1. B
2. D
3. D
4. B
5. E

Problem III

16	Accounting equation	14	GAAS
52	Accounts payable	54	Generally Accepted Accounting Principles
26	Accounts receivable	11	Generally Accepted Auditing Standards
4	AcSB	38	Going concern principle
36	ASB	3	IASC
51	Assets	27	Income statement
12	Balance sheet	49	Liabilities
39	Balance sheet equation	37	Monetary unit principle
41	Business activities	13	Natural business year
6	Business entity principle	29	Net assets
21	Business events	42	Net income
44	Business transaction	2	Net loss
15	Calendar year	9	Note payable
25	Cash flow statement	33	Objectivity principle
32	CICA Handbook	17	Owner investments
1	Comparability	40	Owner's equity
28	Consistency	45	Owner withdrawals
50	Cost principle	5	Profit
19	Creditors	23	Relevance
35	Debtors	53	Reliability
31	Economic consideration	18	Revenue recognition principle
48	Equity	46	Revenues
8	Expenses	34	Source documents
30	Event	20	Statement of owner's equity
47	Financial statements	43	Statement of financial position
22	Fiscal year	24	Transaction
10	GAAP	7	Withdrawal

Problem IV

1. using up (consuming)
2. accounts receivable; accounts payable
3. Assets; Liabilities; Owner's Equity; accounting
4. net income (profit); net loss; income statement
5. date; assets; liabilities; equity
6. assets; liabilities
7. liabilities
8. creditors; debtors
9. business entity; owner; owners
10. cash, operating; investing; financing
11. net income or net loss; new investments by the owner; withdrawals
12. costs; going-concern; continuing concern; earned

Problem V

	Cash	Accounts + Receivable +	Prepaid Rent	+ Supplies	Office + Equipment =	= Liabilities + Accounts Payable +	Owner's Equity J. Leung, Capital
	$10,000	$0	$0	$1,000	$12,000	$0	$23,000
1.	-4,000		+4,000				
	6,000	0	4,000	1,000	12,000	0	23,000
2.	-750			+750			
	5,250	0	4,000	1,750	12,000	0	23,000
3.	+1,800						+1,800
	7,050	0	4,000	1,750	12,000	0	24,800
4.					+1,500	+1,500	
	7,050	0	4,000	1,750	13,500	1,500	24,800
5.		+1,600					+1,600
	7,050	1,600	4,000	1,750	13,500	1,500	26,400
6.	-1,500					-1,500	
	5,550	1,600	4,000	1,750	13,500	0	26,400
7.	+1,600	-1,600					
	7,150	0	4,000	1,750	13,500	0	26,400
8.	-800						-800
	6,350	0	4,000	1,750	13,500	0	25,600
9.	-3,000						-3,000
	$3,350	$0	$4,000	$1,750	$13,500	$0	$22,600

a. Yes

b. Yes

c. an error had been made

d. cash

e. an account receivable

f. cash; legal work

g. revenue recognition (or realization); earned; cash; noncash assets

Learning Objective 1:

Explain the accounting cycle.

Summary

The accounting cycle includes the steps in preparing financial statements for users that are repeated each reporting period.

Learning Objective 2:

Describe an account, its use, and its relationship to the ledger.

Summary

An account is a detailed record of increases and decreases in a specific asset, liability, or equity item. Information is taken from accounts, analyzed, summarized, and presented in useful reports and financial statements for users.

Learning Objective 3:

Define debits and credits and explain their role in double-entry accounting.

Summary

Debit refers to left, and credit refers to right. The following table summarizes debit and credit effects by account type:

	Assets =	Liabilities +	Owner's Equity			
			Owner's Capital	Owner's Withdrawals	Revenues	Expenses
Increases	Debits	Credits	Credits	Debits	Credits	Debits
Decreases	Credits	Debits	Debits	Credits	Debits	Credits

Double-entry accounting means every transaction affects at least two accounts. The total amount debited must equal the total amount credited for each transaction. The system for recording debits and credits follows from the accounting equation. The debit side is the normal balance for assets, owner's withdrawals, and expenses, and the credit side is the normal balance for liabilities, owner's capital, and revenues.

Learning Objective 4:

Describe a chart of accounts and its relationship to the ledger.

Summary

A ledger is a record containing all accounts used by a company. This is what is referred to as *the books*. The chart of accounts is a listing of all accounts and usually includes an identification number assigned to each account.

Learning Objective 5:

Analyze the impact of transactions on accounts.

Summary

We analyze transactions using the concepts of double-entry accounting. This analysis is performed by determining a transaction's effects on accounts. These effects are recorded in journals and posted to accounts in the ledger.

Learning Objective 6:

Record transactions in a journal and post entries to a ledger.

Summary

We record transactions in a journal to give a record of their effects. Each entry in a journal is posted to the accounts in the ledger. This provides information in accounts that is used to produce financial statements. Balance column ledger accounts are widely used and include columns for debits, credits and the account balance after each entry.

Learning Objective 7:

Prepare and explain the use of a trial balance.

Summary

A trial balance is a list of accounts in the ledger showing the debit and credit balances in separate columns. The trial balance is a convenient summary of the ledger's contents and is useful in preparing financial statements. It reveals errors of the kind that produce unequal debit and credit account balances.

Chapter Outline

I.   **The Accounting Cycle**

    A. The steps in preparing financial statements for users are repeated each reporting period. They are: analyze transactions, journalize, post, prepare unadjusted trial balance, adjust, prepare adjusted trial balance, prepare statements, close, and prepare post-closing trial balance.

II.   **Accounts and Double-Entry Accounting**

    A. *An account* is a detailed record of increases and decreases in a specific asset, liability, or equity item.

    B. A *ledger* is a record containing all accounts used by a business.

    C. Separate accounts are kept for each type of asset, liability, and equity item. Examples:

        1. *Assets:* are resources controlled by an organization that have current and future benefits. They have value and are used in the operations of the business to create revenue. Some asset accounts are:

            a. Cash: includes coins, currency, cheques, money orders, and chequing account balances.

            b. Accounts Receivables: occur when services are performed for or goods are sold to customers in return for promises to pay in the future, transactions are *on credit* or *on account*. Accounts receivable are increased by services performed or goods sold on credit and decreased by customer payments.

            c. Note Receivable (or a promissory note): an unconditional written promise to pay a definite sum of money on demand or on a defined future date(s).

            d. Prepaid Expenses: contain payments made for assets that are to be used in the near future. As these assets are used up, the costs of the used assets become expenses. Examples: office supplies, store supplies, prepaid insurance, prepaid rent.

            e. Equipment: assets used in the operations of a business for more than one accounting period, such as computers, printers, desks, chairs, counters, showcases and cash registers.

            f. Buildings: assets owned by an organization that can provide space for a store, office, warehouse, or factory. Buildings are assets because they provide benefits.

            g. Land: cost is separated from the cost of buildings to provide more useful information

2. *Liabilities:* are obligations to transfer assets or provide services to other entities. Examples:

    a. Accounts payable: occur with the purchase of merchandise, supplies, equipment, or services made by a promise to pay later.

    b. Note payable: occur when an organization formally recognizes a promise to pay by signing a promissory note.

    c. Unearned revenues: result when customers pay in advance for products or services. These are liabilities because a service or product is owed to a customer. It will be earned when the service or product is delivered in the future.

    d. Other liability accounts: wages payable, taxes payable, and interest payable.

3. *Equity accounts:*

    a. Owner capital: records owner investments; identified by using the owner's name.

    b. Owner withdrawals: an account with the owner's name and the word *Withdrawals*.

    c. Revenues: examples are Sales, Commissions Earned, Rent Revenue, and Interest Earned.

    d. Expenses: examples are Advertising Expense, Store Supplies Expense, Rent Expense, and Utilities Expense.

C. A T-account is learning tool that represents an account in the ledger. It shows the effects of individual transactions on specific accounts. Its shape looks like the letter T. The format includes:

1. The account title on top, the left or debit side (*Dr.*), and the right or credit side (*Cr.*).

D. Account Balance – is the difference between the increases and decreases recorded in an account. To determine the balance, we:

1. Compute the total increases shown on one side (including the beginning balance)

2. Compute the total decreases shown on the other side

3. Subtract the sum of the decreases from the sum of the increases, and

4. Calculate the account balance

Chapter Outline

III. **Debits and Credits**

Debit side: the left side of a T-account: abbreviated Dr. To enter amounts on the left side of an account is to *debit* the account.

Credit side: the right side of a T-account: abbreviated Cr. To enter amounts on the right side of an account is to *credit* the account.

A. Double-entry accounting means every transaction affects and is recorded in at least two accounts. *The total amount debited must equal the total amount credited*. Therefore, the sum of the debits for all entries must equal the sum of the credits for all entries. The sum of the debit account balances must equal the sum of the credit account balances.

B. The system for recording debits and credits balances follows the accounting equation.
   1. *Assets:* debit for increases; credit for decreases.
   2. *Liabilities and owner's equity*: debit for decreases; credit for increases.
   3. *Owner's equity:* debit for decreases; credit for increases.
      a. Owner's capital: investments by the owner are credited to owner's capital because they increase equity.
      b. Revenues: are credited to revenues accounts because they increase equity.
      c. Expenses: are debited to expense accounts because they decrease equity.
      d. Owner's withdrawals: are debited to owner's withdrawals because they decrease equity.
   4. The normal balance of each account refers to the debit or credit side where increases are recorded.

IV. **Chart of Accounts**
   1. Ledger: the collation of all accounts for an information system.
   2. Chart of accounts: a list of all accounts used in the ledger by a company.

Chapter Outline

Notes

V. Analyzing Transactions

Step one: Analyze a transaction and its source document(s).

Step two: Apply double-entry accounting to identify the effect of a transaction on account balances.

1. Investment by owner -- debit Cash and credit owner's capital
2. Purchase supplies for cash – debit Supplies and credit Cash
3. Purchase furniture and supplies on credit including a promissory note – debit Supplies and debit Furniture and credit Accounts Payable and Notes Payable
4. Services rendered for cash – debit Cash and credit Consulting Revenue
5. Payment of expense in cash – debit Rent Expense and credit Cash
6. Payment of expense in cash – debit Salaries Expense and credit Cash
7. Service contract signed for a future period – no economic exchange, therefore no journal entry
8. Services and rental revenues rendered on credit – debit Accounts Receivable and credit Consulting Revenue and Rental Revenue
9. Receipt of cash on account – debit Cash and credit Accounts Receivable
10. Partial payment of accounts payable – debit Accounts Payable and credit Cash
11. Withdrawal of cash by owner – debit owner's withdrawals and credit Cash
12. Receipt of cash for future services – debit Cash and credit Unearned Consulting Revenue
13. Payment of cash for future insurance coverage – debit Prepaid Insurance and credit Cash
14. Payment of expense in cash – debit Utilities Expense and credit Cash
15. Payment of expense in cash – debit Salaries Expense and credit Cash

VI. Recording and Posting Transactions

A. *Journalizing* is the process of recording transactions in a journal. Record transactions in a journal to avoid the potential for error and the difficulty in tracking mistakes. A *journal* gives a complete record of each transaction in one place, directly linking the debits and credits for each transaction.

B. *Posting* is the process of transferring entries from the journal to the ledger. *This step occurs after debits and credits for each*

© *McGraw-Hill Ryerson, Inc., 2005*

3-34 *Fundamental Accounting Principles, 11th Canadian Edition transaction are entered into a journal.*

Chapter Outline

VII. **Trial Balance**

A. A trial balance is a list of accounts and their balances at a point in time. Account balances are reported in the debit or credit columns. The sum of debit account balances must equal the sum of credit account balances.

B. The trial balance tests the equality of the debit and credit account balances. The trial balance is also used as an internal report for preparing financial statements.

C. Preparing a trial balance involves five steps:

1. Identify each account balance from the ledger.

2. List each account and its balance. Enter debit balances in the debit column and credit balances in the credit column.

3. Compute the total of debit balances.

4. Compute the total of credit balances.

5. Verify that total debit balances equal total credit balances.

D. When a trial balance does not balance (the its columns are not equal), one or more errors exist. These errors often arise from one of the following steps in the accounts process:

1. preparing journal entries

2. posting entries to the ledger

3. computing account balances

4. copying account balances to the trial balance

5. totalling the trial balance columns.

Any errors must be found and corrected before preparing the financial statements.

THREE PARTS OF AN ACCOUNT

(1) ACCOUNT TITLE

Left Side Called (2) DEBIT	Right Side called (3) CREDIT

Rules for using accounts

Accounts have <u>balance</u> sides (Debit or Credit)

To <u>increase</u> any account, use the balance side

To <u>decrease</u> any account, use the <u>side opposite</u> the balance

Finding account balances

If total debits = total credits, the account balance is zero.

If total <u>debits are greater</u> than total credits, the account has a <u>debit balance</u> equal to the difference of the two totals.

If total <u>credits are greater</u> than total debits, the account has a <u>credit balance</u> equal to the difference of the two totals.

REAL ACCOUNTS

ALL ACCOUNTS HAVE BALANCE SIDES

BALANCE SIDES FOR ASSETS, LIABILITIES, AND
EQUITY ACCOUNTS ARE BASED ON
THE SIDE OF EQUATION THEY ARE ON.

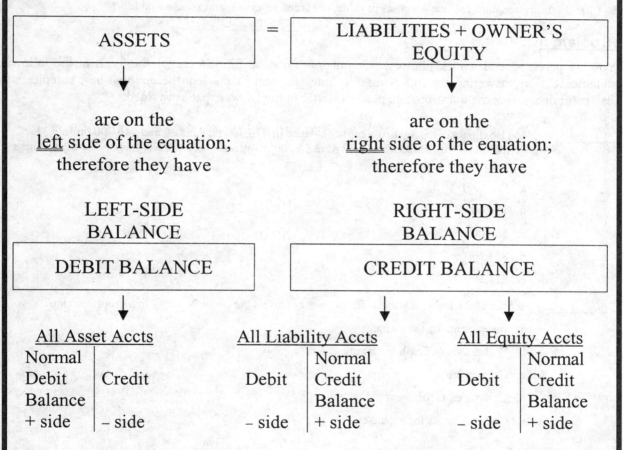

ASSETS	=	LIABILITIES + OWNER'S EQUITY

are on the
left side of the equation;
therefore they have

are on the
right side of the equation;
therefore they have

LEFT-SIDE BALANCE	RIGHT-SIDE BALANCE
DEBIT BALANCE	CREDIT BALANCE

All Asset Accts		All Liability Accts		All Equity Accts	
Normal Debit Balance + side	Credit – side	Debit – side	Normal Credit Balance + side	Debit – side	Normal Credit Balance + side

*In a sole proprietorship, there is only one owner's equity account, which is called capital. For that reason, the terms equity and capital are often used interchangeably. When corporations are discussed in detail, you will learn many (shareholder's) equity accounts. Owner's equity is an account classification like assets. Owner's name, capital, is the account title.

Problem I

The following statements are either true or false. Place a (T) in the parentheses before each true statement and an (F) before each false statement.

1. ( ) Debits are used to record increases in assets, withdrawals, and expenses.

2. ( ) The process of recording transactions in a journal is called posting.

3. ( ) In double-entry accounting, all errors are avoided by being sure that debits and credits are equal when transactions are recorded.

4. ( ) The cost of renting an office during the current period is an expense; however, the cost of renting an office six periods in advance is an asset.

5. ( ) Liability accounts include accounts payable, unearned revenues, and notes payable.

Problem II

You are given several words, phrases, or numbers to choose from in completing each of the following statements or in answering the following questions. In each case select the one that best completes the statement or answers the question, and place its letter in the answer space provided.

_____ 1. Joe Boxling's company had a capital balance of $33,400 on June 30 and $46,700 on July 31. Withdrawals for the month of July were $5,200. How much was the Net Income for the business during July?

 a. ($8,100)

 b. $5,200

 c. $8,100

 d. $13,300

 e. $18,500

_____ 2. Which of the following transactions does not affect the owner's equity in a proprietorship?

 a. Investments by the owner.

 b. Withdrawals of cash by the owner.

 c. Cash receipts for revenues.

 d. Cash receipts for unearned revenues.

 e. Cash payments for expenses.

_____ 3. A ledger is:

 a. A book of original entry in which the effects of transactions are first recorded.

 b. The collection of all accounts used by a business.

 c. A book of original entry in which any type of transaction can be recorded.

 d. A book of special journals.

 e. An account with debit and credit columns and a third column for showing the balance of the account.

_____4. The following transactions occurred during the month of October:

1) Paid $1,500 cash for store equipment.

2) Paid $1,000 in partial payment for supplies purchased 30 days previously.

3) Paid October's utility bill of $600.

4) Paid $1,200 to owner of business for his personal use.

5) Paid $1,400 salary of office employee for October.

What was the total amount of expenses during October?

a. $3,000.

b. $4,500.

c. $2,000.

d. $3,500.

e. $5,700.

_____5. The journal entry to record the completion of legal work for a client on credit and billing the client $1,700 for the services rendered would be:

a. Accounts Receivable 1,700

    Unearned Legal Fees... 1,700

b. Legal Fees Earned 1,700

    Accounts Receivable 1,700

c. Accounts Payable 1,700

    Legal Fees Earned 1,700

d. Legal Fees Earned...1,700

    Sales... 1,700

e. Accounts Receivable 1,700

    Legal Fees Earned 1,700

Problem III

Following are the first ten transactions completed by A. P. Larsen's new business called Larsen's Repair Shop:

  a.   Started the business with a cash deposit of $4,000 to a bank account in the name of the business.
  b.   Paid three months' rent in advance on the shop space, $1,500.
  c.   Purchased repair equipment for cash, $2,200.
  d.   Completed repair work for customers and collected cash, $1,200.
  e.   Purchased additional repair equipment on credit from Lenney Company, $575.
  f.   Completed repair work on credit for Joe Whalen, $250.
  g.   Paid Lenney Company $300 of the amount owed from transaction (e).
  h.   Paid the local radio station $150 for an announcement of the shop opening.
  i.   Joe Whalen paid for the work completed in transaction (f).
  j.   Withdrew $350 cash from the bank for A. P. Larsen to pay personal expenses.

Required

1.   Record the transactions directly in the T-accounts that follow. Use the transaction letters to identify the amounts in the accounts.

2.   Prepare a trial balance as of the current date using the form that follows.

Cash	Accounts Payable

	A. P. Larsen, Capital

Accounts Receivable	A. P. Larsen, Withdrawals

Prepaid Rent	Repair Services Revenue

Repair Equipment	Advertising Expense

Fundamental Accounting Principles, 11th Canadian Edition

LARSEN'S REPAIR SHOP

Trial Balance

_____, 20____

Problem IV

Journalize the following transactions and post to the accounts that follow.

a. On November 5 of the current year, Megan Lear invested $1,700 in cash, and equipment having a fair value of $800, to start a decorating business.

b. On November 6, the business purchased additional equipment for $425 cash.

© McGraw-Hill Ryerson, Inc., 2005

GENERAL JOURNAL

DATE	ACCOUNT TITLES ANDEXPLANATION	P.R.	DEBIT	CREDIT

Fundamental Accounting Principles, 11ᵗʰ Canadian Edition

GENERAL LEDGER

Cash   Account No. 101

DATE	EXPLANATION	P.R.	DEBIT	CREDIT

Equipment   Account No. 163

DATE	EXPLANATION	P.R.	DEBIT	CREDIT

Megan Lear, Capital   Account No. 301

DATE	EXPLANATION	P.R.	DEBIT	CREDIT

© McGraw-Hill Ryerson, Inc., 2005

Problem V

Many of the important ideas and concepts discussed in Chapter 3 are reflected in the following list of key terms. Test your understanding of these terms by matching the appropriate definition with the terms. Record the number identifying the most appropriate definition in the blank space next to each term.

	Account		Journalizing
	Account balance		Ledger
	Accounting cycle		Normal balance
	Accounts payable		Note receivable
	Accounts receivable		Note payable
	Balance column ledger account		Posting
	Chart of accounts		Posting Reference (PR) column
	Compound journal entry		Prepaid expenses
	Credit		Promissory Note
	Debit		T-account
	Double-entry accounting		Transposition error
	General Journal		Trial balance
	Journal		Unearned revenues

1. When services are performed for or goods are sold to customers in return for promises to pay in the future, this is recorded. These transactions are said to be on credit or on account. These are increased by services performed or goods sold on credit and decreased by customer payments.

2. An entry that increases asset, expense, and owner's withdrawals accounts or decreases liability, owner's capital, and revenue accounts; recorded on the left side of a T-account.

3. A simple characterization of an account form used as a helpful tool in showing the effects of transactions and events on specific accounts.

4. Transfer journal entry information to ledger accounts.

5. Liabilities created when customers pay in advance for products or services; created when cash is received before revenues are earned; satisfied by delivering the products or services in the future.

6. The difference between the increases (including the beginning balance) and decreases recorded in an account.

7. A journal entry that affects at least three accounts.

8. The most flexible type of journal; can be used to record any kind of transaction.

9. A place or location within an accounting system in which the increases and decreases in a specific asset, liability, or equity are recorded and stored.

10. A record where transactions are recorded before they are recorded in accounts; amounts are posted from the journal to the ledger; also called the book of original entry.

11. The debit or credit side on which an account increases. For example, assets increase with debits, therefore the normal balance for an asset is a debit. Revenues increase with credits, therefore a credit is the normal balance for a revenue account.

12. An account with debit and credit columns for recording entries and a third column showing the balance of the account after each entry is posted.

13. An asset account containing payments made for assets that are not to be used until later.

14. Error due to two digits being switched or transposed within a number.

15. Obligations that arise when a promise to pay later is made in connection with purchases of merchandise, supplies, or equipment.

16. An entry that decreases asset, expense, and owner's withdrawals accounts or increases liability, owner's capital, and revenue accounts; recorded on the right side of a T-account.

17. A column in journals where individual account numbers are entered when entries are posted to the ledger. A column in ledgers where journal page numbers are entered when entries are posted.

18. An unconditional written promise to pay a definite sum of money on demand or on a defined future date(s); also called a promissory note.

19. A list of all accounts used by a company; includes the identification number assigned to each account.

20. A list of accounts and their balances at a point in time; the total debit balances should equal the total credit balances.

21. The steps repeated each reporting period for the purpose of preparing financial statements for users.

22. An accounting system where every transaction affects and is recorded in at least two accounts; the sum of the debits for all entries must equal the sum of the credits for all entries.

23. Recording transactions in a journal.

24. Obligations that arise when an organization formally recognizes a promise to pay by signing a promissory note.

Problem VI

Complete the following by filling in the blanks.

1. Assets are resources controlled by an organization that have _____ and _____ benefits. They have value and are used in the operations of the business to create _____ .

2. A _____ is an amount of cash that the business is expecting to receive in the future. When services are performed for or goods are sold to customers in return for promises to pay in the future, a(n) ˙_____ is recorded. A _____ , or a _____ , is an unconditional written promise to pay a definite sum of money on demand or on a defined future date.

3. A _____ is an obligation to transfer assets or provide services to other entities. Purchases of merchandise, supplies, equipment or services made by an oral or implied promise to pay later produce _____ _____ . _____ _____ is satisfied by delivering products or services in the future.

4. Four transactions that affect equity are _____ , _____ , _____ , and _____ .

5. The process of recording transactions in a journal is called _____ . The process of transferring journal entry information to the ledger is called _____ .

6. The _____ is a helpful learning tool that represents an account in the ledger.

7. Notes receivable and prepaid insurance are examples of a(n) _____ account. Unearned revenues and interest payable are examples of a(n) _____ account.

8. Balances of _____ and _____ accounts flow into the income statement. Then, net income from the income statement and balances from _____ and _____ accounts flow into the statement of changes in owner's equity. Then, ending owner's equity and balances from _____ and _____ accounts flow into the balance sheet.

9.   a. Increases to assets are recorded as _____ ; decreases as _____ .

   b. Increases to liabilities are recorded as _____ ; decreases as _____ .

   c. Increases to owner's capital are recorded as _____ .

   d. Increases to revenues are recorded as _____ .

   e. Increases to expenses are recorded as _____ .

   f. Increases to owner's withdrawals are recorded as _____ .

10. The steps in preparing a trial balance are: _____

   (1) _____
   _____

   (2) _____
   _____

   (3) _____
   _____

   (4) _____
   _____

   (5) _____
   _____

11. The _____ _____ of each account refers to the debit or credit side where increases are recorded.

12. A trial balance that balances is not absolute proof that no errors were made because
_____ .

13. One frequent error that is made is called a _____ , which occurs when two digits within a number are switched. This type of error probably has occurred if the difference between the two trial balance columns is evenly divisible by _____ .

Solutions for Chapter 3

Problem I

1. T
2. F
3. F
4. T
5. T

Problem II

1. E
2. D
3. B
4. C
5. E

Problem III

Cash			
(a)	4,000.00	(b)	1,500.00
(d)	1,200.00	(c)	2,200.00
(i)	250.00	(g)	300.00
		(h)	150.00
		(j)	350.00

Repair Equipment	
(c)	2,200.00
(e)	575.00

A. P. Larsen, Withdrawals	
(j)	350.00

Accounts Receivable			
(f)	250.00	(i)	250.00

Accounts Payable			
(g)	300.00	(e)	575.00

Repair Services Revenue			
		(d)	1,200.00
		(f)	250.00

Prepaid Rent	
(b)	1,500.00

A. P. Larsen, Capital	
(a)	4,000.00

Advertising Expense	
(h)	150.00

LARSEN'S REPAIR SHOP
Trial Balance
(Current Date)

Cash	$ 950.00	
Prepaid rent	1,500.00	
Repair equipment	2,775.00	
Accounts payable		$ 275.00
P. L. Wheeler, capital		4,000.00
P. L. Wheeler, withdrawals	350.00	
Repair services revenue		1,450.00
Advertising expense	150.00	
Totals	$5,725.00	$5,725.00

Problem IV

GENERAL JOURNAL

DATE	ACCOUNT TITLES AND EXPLANATION	P.R.	DEBIT	CREDIT
20— Nov. 5	Cash	101	1 7 0 0 00	
	Equipment	163	8 0 0 00	
	Megan Lear, Capital	301		2 5 0 0 00
	Owner's initial investment.			
6	Equipment	163	4 2 5 00	
	Cash	101		4 2 5 00
	Purchased office equipment			

GENERAL LEDGER

Cash   Account No. 101

DATE	EXPLANATION	P.R.	DEBIT	CREDIT	BALANCE
20— Nov. 5		G-1	1 7 0 0 00		1 7 0 0 00
6		G-1		4 2 5 00	1 2 7 5 00

Equipment   Account No. 163

DATE	EXPLANATION	P.R.	DEBIT	CREDIT	BALANCE
20— Nov. 5		G-1	8 0 0 00		8 0 0 00
6		G-1	4 2 5 00		1 2 2 5 00

Megan Lear, Capital   Account No. 301

DATE	EXPLANATION	P.R.	DEBIT	CREDIT	BALANCE
20— Nov. 5		G-1		2 5 0 0 00	2 5 0 0 00

Problem V

9	Account	23	Journalizing
6	Account balance	26	Ledger
21	Accounting cycle	11	Normal balance
15	Accounts payable	18	Note receivable
1	Accounts receivable	24	Note payable
12	Balance column ledger account	4	Posting
19	Chart of accounts	17	Posting Reference (PR) column
7	Compound journal entry	13	Prepaid expenses
16	Credit	25	Promissory Note
2	Debit	3	T-account
22	Double-entry accounting	14	Transposition error
8	General Journal	20	Trial balance
10	Journal	5	Unearned revenues

Problem VI

1. current, future, revenue

2. receivable, account receivable, note receivable, promissory note

3. liability, account payable, unearned revenue

4. investment by the owner, withdrawals by the owner, revenues, expenses

5. journalizing, posting

6. T-account

7. asset, liability

8. revenue, expense; capital, withdrawals; asset, liability

9. (a) debits, credits; (b) credits, debits; (c) credits; (d) credits; (e) debits; (f) debits

10. (1) Identify each account balance from the ledger.

    (2) List each account and its balance (in the same order as the Chart of Accounts). Debit balances are entered in the Debit column and credit balances in the Credit column.

    (3) Compute the total of debit balances

    (4) Compute the total of credit balances

    (5) Verify that total debit balances equal total credit balances.

11. normal balance

12. some types of errors do not create unequal debits and credits

13. transposition, nine

CHAPTER 4

ADJUSTING ACCOUNTS FOR FINANCIAL STATEMENTS

Learning Objective 1:

Describe the purpose of adjusting accounts at the end of a period.

Summary

After external transactions are recorded, several accounts in the ledger often need adjusting for their balances to be correct because internal transactions remain unrecorded. The purpose of adjusting accounts at the end of a period is to recognize unrecorded revenues and expenses.

Learning Objective 2:

Explain how the time period, matching, and revenue recognition principles affect the adjusting process.

Summary

The value of information is often linked to its timeliness so accounting systems prepare periodic reports at regular intervals such as a month, a three-month quarter, or a year for periodic reporting. Adjusts are made so that revenues and expenses are recognized as they occur and matched to the proper period.

Learning Objective 3:

Explain accrual accounting and cash basis accounting and how accrual accounting adds to the usefulness of financial statements.

Summary

Accrual accounting recognizes revenue when earned and expenses when incurred, not necessarily when cash inflows and outflows occur. Cash basis accounting recognizes revenues when cash is received and expenses when cash is paid; it is not in accordance with GAAP.

Learning Objective 4:

Prepare and explain adjusting entries for prepaid expenses, amortization, unearned revenues, accrued expenses, and accrued revenues.

Summary

Prepaid expenses, an asset, refer to items paid for in advance of receiving their benefits. As this asset is used, its cost becomes an expense.

Dr.   Expense

    Cr.   Prepaid

To adjust prepaid for amount used.

Amortization is the expense created by spreading the cost of capital assets over the periods these assets are used. Accumulated Amortization, a contra asset account, is credited to track the total amount of the capital asset used.

Dr.   Amortization Expense

    Cr.   Accumulated Amortization

To adjust for amortization.

Unearned revenues, a liability, refer to cash received in advance of providing products and services. As products and services are provided, the amount of unearned revenues becomes earned revenues.

Dr.   Unearned Revenue

    Cr.   Revenue

To adjust for unearned revenue that is earned.

Accrued expenses are costs incurred in a period that are unpaid and unrecorded.

Dr.   Expense

    Cr.   Liability

To adjust for unrecorded and unpaid expenses.

Accrued revenues are revenues earned in a period that are unrecorded and not yet collected.

Dr.   Receivable

    Cr.   Revenue

To adjust for unrecorded revenues not yet collected.

Learning Objective 5:

Explain how accounting adjustments link to financial statements.

Summary

Accounting adjustments bring an asset or liability account balance to its correct amount and update related expense or revenue accounts. Every adjusting entry affects one or more income statement accounts *and* one or more balance sheet accounts. An adjusting entry never affects cash. Adjustments are necessary for transactions that extend over more than one period. Exhibit 4.20 summarizes financial statement links by type of adjustment.

Learning Objective 6:

Explain and prepare an adjusted trial balance.

Summary

An adjusted trial balance is a list of accounts and balances prepared after adjusting entries are recorded and posted to the ledger. Financial statements are often prepared from the adjusted trial balance.

Learning Objective 7:

Prepare financial statements from an adjusted trial balance.

Summary

We can prepare financial statements directly from the adjusted trial balance that includes all account balances. Revenue and expense balances are transferred to the income statement and statement of owner's equity. Asset, liability and owner's equity balances are transferred to the balance sheet. We usually prepare statements in the following order: income statement, statement of owner's equity, and balance sheet.

Learning Objective 8 (Appendix 4A):

Explain and prepare correcting entries.

Summary

A correcting entry is required when an error in a journal entry is not discovered until after it has been posted. The correcting entry can be done in one of two ways: the incorrect portion of the entry can be corrected, or the entire incorrect entry can be reversed and the correct entry recorded; both methods accomplish the same result.

Learning Objective 9 (Appendix 4B):

Identify and explain two alternatives in accounting for prepaids and unearned revenues.

Summary

It is acceptable to charge all prepaid expenses to expense accounts when they are purchased. When this is done, adjusting entries must transfer any unexpired amounts from expense accounts to asset accounts. It is also acceptable to credit all unearned revenues to revenue accounts when cash is received. In this case the adjusting entries must transfer any unearned amounts from revenue accounts to unearned revenue accounts.

Chapter Outline

I. Purpose of Adjusting

At the end of the period, after external transactions are recorded, several accounts in the ledger need adjustment for their balances to appear in financial statements. This need arises because internal transactions and events remain unrecorded.

II. GAAP and the Adjusting Process

A. The Accounting Period—Accounting systems need to prepare periodic reports at regular intervals.

   1. Time period principle—assumes that an organization's activities can be divided into specific time periods such as a month, a three-month quarter, or a year.

   2. Time periods covered by statements are called accounting periods or reports periods.

B. Recognizing Revenues and Expenses—two generally accepted accounting principles are used:

   1. The revenue recognition principle, and

   2. The matching principle: aims to report expenses in the same accounting period as the revenues they helped to earn.

III. Accrual Basis Compared to Cash Basis

   1. Accrual basis accounting—revenues and expenses are recognized or recorded when earned or incurred regardless of when cash is received or paid. Based on the revenue recognition principle.

   2. Cash basis accounting—recognizes revenues and expenses when *cash* is received or paid. Not consistent with GAAP.

IV. Adjusting Accounts—An adjusting entry is recorded at the end of an accounting period to bring an asset or liability account balance to its proper amount. This entry also updates the related expense or revenue account.

A. Framework for adjustments—group adjustments by their timing of cash receipt or payment in comparison to when they are recognized as revenues or expenses.

B. Adjusting Prepaid Expenses

1. Prepaid expenses - items *paid for* in advance of receiving their benefits. Prepaid expenses are assets. As these assets are used, their costs become expenses.

2. Adjusting entries for prepaids involve increasing (debiting) expenses and decreasing (crediting) assets.

3. Common prepaid items: insurance, supplies, and rent.

C. Adjusting for Amortization

1. Capital assets include long-term tangible assets (such as plant and equipment) that are used to produce and sell products and services and, intangible assets (such as patents) that convey the right to use a product or process. These assets are expected to provide benefits for more than one period.

2. Amortization is the process of computing expense from matching (or allocating) the cost of capital assets over their expected useful lives. Several methods can be used to calculate the amortization. The straight-line amortization method allocates equal amounts of an asset's net cost over its estimated useful life.

3. Accumulated Amortization is recorded in a contra asset account—an account linked with another account and having an opposite normal balance. It is reported as a subtraction from the other account's balance. The cost of the asset less its accumulated amortization is the *book value* of the asset. The *market value* of an asset is the amount it can be sold for. Market value is not tied to the book value of an asset.

D. Adjusting Unearned Revenues

1. Unearned Revenues are liabilities created when cash is received in advance of providing products and services.

2. Adjusting entries for unearned revenues involve increasing (crediting) revenues and decreasing (debiting) unearned revenues.

E. Adjusting Accrued Expenses

1. Accrued Expenses are costs incurred in a period that are both unpaid and unrecorded.

2. Adjusting entries for recording accrued expenses involve increasing (debiting) expenses and increasing (crediting) liabilities.

3. Common accrued expenses are interest, salaries, rent and taxes.

    F.   Adjusting Accrued Revenues

        1. Accrued Revenues are revenues earned in a period that are both unrecorded and not yet received in cash (or other assets).

        2. Adjusting entries increase (debit) assets and increase (credit) revenues.

        3. Commonly accrued revenues are fees for services and products, interest and rent.

V. Adjustments and Financial Statements—each adjusting entry affects one or more income statement accounts *and* one or more balance sheet accounts. (See text exhibit 4.20 for a summary of adjustments and financial statement links. *Note that adjusting entries related to the framework never affect cash*.)

VI. Adjusted Trial Balance—

    A. Unadjusted trial balance—a listing of accounts and balances prepared *before* adjustments are recorded.

    B. Adjusted trial balance—a listing of accounts and balances prepared *after* adjusting entries are recorded and posted to the ledger.

VII.   **Preparing Financial Statements**—prepare financial statements directly from information in the *adjusted* trial balance. Prepare financial statements in the following order:

    A. Income Statement

    B. Statement of Owner's Equity (uses net income or loss from the income statement).

    C. Balance Sheet (uses ending equity from the statement of owner's equity). Balance Sheets can be prepared in one of two formats:

        1. Account form— lists assets on the left and liabilities and owner's equity on the right side of the balance sheet.

        2. Report form—lists items vertically, placing the assets above the liabilities and the owner's equity.

V.   **Accrual Adjustments in Later Periods**—accrued revenues/expenses of one period generally result in cash receipts/payments in next period.

    A. Paying accrued expenses—Debit the payable for amount previously accrued and credit cash for full amount paid. If the amount paid exceeds amount accrued, the difference is additional expense.

    B. Receiving accrued revenues—Debit cash for the full amount received and credit the receivable for amount previously accrued. If the amount received exceeds amount accrued, the difference is additional revenue.

VIII. **Appendix 4A - Correcting Errors**

    A. Before the error is posted: replace the incorrect information directly

    B. After the error has been posted: correct the error by creating another journal entry.

IX. **Appendix 4B—Alternatives in accounting for Prepaids and Unearned Revenues**

    A. Recording prepaid expenses in expense accounts – if prepaid expenses are originally recorded with debits to expense accounts, adjust at the end of the period by transferring the unused portions from expense accounts to asset accounts.

    B. Recording unearned revenues in revenue accounts – if unearned revenues are originally recorded as credits to revenue accounts, adjust at the end of the period by transferring the unearned portions from revenue accounts to unearned revenue accounts.

    C. Note that the financial statements are identical under either procedure, but the adjusting entries are different.

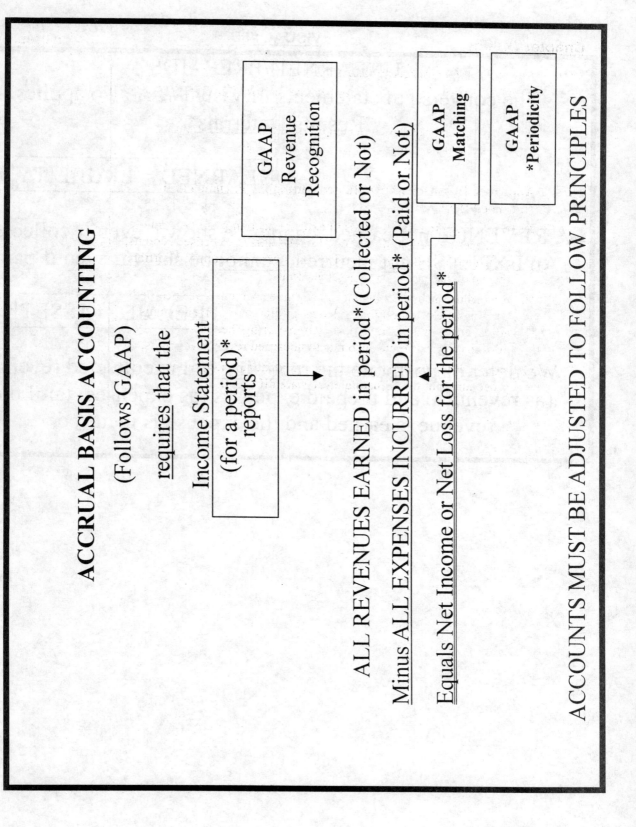

ACCRUAL BASIS ACCOUNTING

(Follows GAAP)

requires that the

Income Statement

(for a period)* reports

| GAAP Revenue Recognition |

ALL REVENUES EARNED in period* (Collected or Not)

Minus ALL EXPENSES INCURRED in period* (Paid or Not)

| GAAP Matching |

Equals Net Income or Net Loss for the period*

| GAAP *Periodicity |

ACCOUNTS MUST BE ADJUSTED TO FOLLOW PRINCIPLES

UNEARNED/PREPAIDS

The converse of statements in Visual #5A also applies.

Results <u>Deferrals</u>*

| UNEARNED = LIABILITY | *

A REVENUE <u>not</u> earned, <u>cannot</u> be shown, even if collected.

An EXPENSE <u>not</u> incurred, <u>cannot</u> be shown, even if paid.

| PREPAID = ASSET | *

*We defer or postpone the <u>reporting</u> of the collected revenues (as revenues) and prepaid expenses (as expenses) until the revenue is earned and the expense is incurred.

VISUAL #6

<table>
<tr><td colspan="3" align="center">ADJUSTMENTS</td></tr>
<tr><td align="center">TYPE</td><td align="center">GENERALIZED*
ENTRY</td><td align="center">AMOUNT</td></tr>
<tr>
<td>1. Prepaid Items or Supplies
   a) initially recorded as assets</td>
<td>Dr. _____ Expense
   Cr. the Asset* acct.</td>
<td>Amount used, or
consumed, or expired</td>
</tr>
<tr>
<td>   b) initially recorded as
     expenses (alternate
     treatment)</td>
<td>Dr. the Asset** acct.
   Cr. _____ Expense</td>
<td>Amount left, or not
consumed, unexpired</td>
</tr>
<tr>
<td>2. Amortization of capital
assets</td>
<td>Dr. Amortization Expense
   Cr. Accumulated
      Amortization</td>
<td>Portion of cost of the
asset allocated to this
period as amortization</td>
</tr>
<tr>
<td>3. Unearned Revenues
   (revenues received in
   advance)
   a) initially recorded as a
     liability (Unearned
     Account)</td>
<td>Dr. Unearned _____
   Cr. the Revenue** acct.</td>
<td>Amount earned to date</td>
</tr>
<tr>
<td>   b) initially recorded as a
     revenue (alternate
     treatment)</td>
<td>Dr. the Revenue** acct.
   Cr. Unearned_____</td>
<td>Amount still <u>not</u>
earned</td>
</tr>
<tr>
<td>4. Accrued Expenses
   (Expenses <u>incurred</u> but not
   yet recorded)</td>
<td>Dr. _____ Expense
   Cr. _____ Payable</td>
<td>Amount accrued</td>
</tr>
<tr>
<td>5. Accrued Revenues
   (Revenues <u>earned</u> but not
   yet recorded)</td>
<td>Dr. _____ Receivable
   Cr. the Revenue** acct.</td>
<td>Amount accrued</td>
</tr>
</table>

  *Notice (1) Each adjustment affects a Balance Sheet Account and an Income
    Statement Account (2) <u>CASH</u> is <u>never</u> in an adjustment.
  **Title or account name varies.

Problem I

The following statements are either true or false. Place a (T) in the parentheses before each true statement and an (F) before each false statement.

1. ( ) The effect of a debit to an unearned revenue account and a corresponding credit to a revenue account is to transfer the earned portion of the fee from the liability account to the revenue account.

2. ( ) If the accountant failed to make the end-of-period adjustment to remove from the Prepaid Expense account the amount of expenses incurred, the omission would cause an overstatement of net income.

3. ( ) If accrued interest is not recorded, the result is that interest expense is understated and interest payable is overstated.

4. ( ) Under the accrual basis of accounting, revenues are recognized when they are earned and expenses are matched with revenues.

5. ( ) Amortizing capital assets causes the expense to be recorded when the asset is purchased.

Problem II

You are given several words, phrases, or numbers to choose from in completing each of the following statements or in answering the following questions. In each case select the one that best completes the statement or answers the question and place its letter in the answer space provided.

_____ 1. Time periods covered by statements are called:
   a. seasonal periods.
   b. fiscal years.
   c. operating cycles of a business.
   d. accounting periods.
   e. natural business years.

_____ 2. J Company paid in advance $300 for six months of insurance on the business. At the end of the first month, the journal entry to record the expense would be:
   a. Insurance Expense 300
          Cash 300
   b. Prepaid Insurance 300
          Cash... 300
   c. Insurance Expense 50
          Prepaid Insurance 50
   d. Prepaid Insurance..50
          Insurance Expense 50
   e. No entry should be made until the salaries are actually paid.

_____ 3 By the end of the current year, Kurt's business had recorded $32,000 of consulting revenues. In addition to this, consulting work for $540 had been completed but not recorded. The adjusting entry at year-end would be:
   a. Cash 540
          Consulting Revenue 540
   b. Accounts Receivable 540
          Consulting Revenue 540
   c. Consulting Revenue 540
          Accounts Payable 540
   d. Accounts Receivable 32,540
          Consulting Revenue 32,540
   e. No entry should be made until the cash is received.

_____4. On Dec. 1, B & B Security Service collected three months' fees of $6,000 in advance of providing services. The amount was recorded as a credit to Unearned Security Service Fees. They provided the monthly service from that date forward. The Dec. 31st adjustment will require Unearned Service Fees be

    a. Credited for $ 2,000.

    b. Debited for $ 6,000.

    c. Credited for $ 6,000.

    d. Debited for $ 4,000.

    e. Debited for $ 2,000.

_____5. Bud's Restaurant prepares monthly financial statements. On January 31 the balance in the Supplies account was $1,600. During February $2,960 of supplies were purchased and debited to Supplies. What is the adjusting entry on February 28 to account for the supplies assuming a February 28 inventory showed that $1,300 of supplies were on hand?

    a. Supplies Expense..300

           Supplies 300

    b. Supplies..300

           Supplies Expense 300

    c. Supplies...3,260

           Cash 3,260

    d. Supplies Expense...3,260

           Supplies 3,260

    e. Some other entry.

_____6. Jay's Delivery Services purchased equipment costing $15,000. The equipment was expected to have a useful life of 6 years. At the end of the 6 years, the equipment was expected to be sold for $3,000. Using straight-line amortization, the adjusting entry to amortize the equipment at the end of the first year would be:

    a. Amortization Expense 2,500

           Accumulated Amortization 2,500

    b. Amortization Expense 2,500

           Equipment... 2,500

    c. Amortization Expense 2,000

           Accumulated Amortization 2,000

    d. Amortization Expense 2,000

           Equipment... 2,000

    e. Some other entry.

Problem III

Many of the important ideas and concepts discussed in Chapter 4 are reflected in the following list of key terms. Test your understanding of these terms by matching the appropriate definitions with the terms. Record the number identifying the most appropriate definition in the blank space next to each term.

	Accounting form balance sheet		External transactions
	Accounting period		Intangible assets
	Accrual basis accounting		Interim financial reports
	Accrued expenses		Internal transactions
	Accrued revenues		Market value of an asset
	Adjusted trial balance		Matching principle
	Adjusting entry		Property, plant and equipment
	Amortization		Prepaid expense
	Book value of an asset		Report form balance sheet
	Capital assets		Reporting period
	Cash basis accounting		Straight-line amortization method
	Contra account		Time-period principle
	Correcting entries		Unadjusted trial balance
	Depreciation		Unearned revenues

1. The approach to preparing financial statements that uses the adjusting process to recognize revenues when earned and expenses when incurred, not when cash is paid or received; the basis for generally accepted accounting principles.

2. Long-lived (capital) assets that have no physical substance but convey a right to use a product or process.

3. Accounting entries made in order to correct errors.

4. Revenues earned in a period that are both unrecorded and not yet received in cash (or other assets); adjusting entries for recording accrued revenues involve increasing (debiting) assets and increasing (crediting) revenues.

5. The expense created by allocating the cost of plant and equipment to the periods in which they are used; represents the expense of using the assets.

6. An accounting period.

7. Include long-term tangible assets, such as plant and equipment, and intangible assets, such as patents. These are expected to provide benefits for more than one period.

8. Amount an asset can be sold for; not tied to the book value of an asset.

9. Cash received in advance of providing products and services.

10. Costs incurred in a period that are both unpaid and unrecorded; adjusting entries for recording accrued expenses involve increasing (debiting) expenses and increasing (crediting) liabilities.

11. Another name for amortization.

12. Exchanges between the entity and some other person or organization.

13. A balance sheet that lists assets on the left and liabilities and owner's equity on the right side of the balance sheet.

14. Exchanges within an organization that can also affect the accounting equation.

15. A listing of accounts and balances prepared after adjustments are recorded and posted to the ledger.

16. A balance sheet that lists items vertically with assets above the liabilities and owner's equity.

17. A listing of accounts and balances prepared before adjustments are recorded and posted to the ledger.

18. Time frame covered by financial statements and other reports.

19. Financial reports covering less than one year usually based on one-, three- or six-month periods.

20. An account linked wit another account having an opposite normal balance; reported as a subtraction from the other account's balance so that more complete information than simply the net amount is provided.

21. A journal entry at the end of an accounting period to bring an asset or liability account balance to its proper amount while also updating the related expense or revenue account.

22. The broad principle that requires expenses to be reported in the same period as the revenues that were earned as a result of the expenses.

23. A broad principle that assumes that an organization's activities can be divided into specific time periods such as months, quarters, or years.

24. Tangible long-lived assets used to produce goods or services.

25. The cost of the asset less its accumulated amortization.

26. Items that are paid for in advance of receiving their benefit. These are assets.

27. Revenues are recognized when cash is received, and expenses are recorded when cash is paid.

28. Allocates equal amounts of an asset's cost to amortizat6ion expense during its useful life.

Problem IV

On October 1 of the current year, Stephanie Ross began a business repairing small appliances. During the month she completed and recorded transactions, resulting in the following unadjusted trial balance.

On October 31, Stephanie Ross decided to adjust her accounts and prepare a balance sheet and an income statement. Her adjustments were:

    a. The amount recorded in Prepaid Rent represented three months' rent paid in advance October 1.

    b. An inventory of office supplies showed $40 of unused office supplies.

    c. The office equipment had depreciated $35 during October.

Required:

1. Complete the worksheet.
2. Journalize and post the adjusting journal entries.
3. From the worksheet, prepare the income statement, statement of owner's equity, and balance sheet.

STEPHANIE ROSS

Worksheet

October 31, 20__

	Unadjusted Trial Balance		Adjustments		Adjusted Trial Balance	
	Dr.	Cr.	Dr.	Cr.	Dr.	Cr.
Cash						
Office supplies						
Prepaid rent						
Office equipment						
Accumulated amortization, office equipment						
Accounts payable						
Stephanie Ross, capital						
Stephanie Ross, withdrawals						
Repair services revenue						
Amortization expense, office equipment						
Rent expense						
Office supplies expense						
Totals						

GENERAL LEDGER

Cash   Account No. 101

DATE	EXPLANATION	P.R.	DEBIT	CREDIT	BALANCE
Oct. 31					2 5 3 0 00

Office Supplies   Account No. 124

DATE	EXPLANATION	P.R.	DEBIT	CREDIT	BALANCE
Oct. 31					7 5 00

Prepaid Rent   Account No. 131

DATE	EXPLANATION	P.R.	DEBIT	CREDIT	BALANCE
Oct. 31					1 5 4 5 00

Office Equipment   Account No. 163

DATE	EXPLANATION	P.R.	DEBIT	CREDIT	BALANCE
Oct. 31					1 6 2 5 00

Accumulated Amortization, Office Equipment   Account No. 164

DATE	EXPLANATION	P.R.	DEBIT	CREDIT	BALANCE

Accounts Payable   Account No. 201

DATE	EXPLANATION	P.R.	DEBIT	CREDIT	BALANCE
Oct.31					7 7 5 00

Stephanie Ross, Capital — Account No. 301

DATE	EXPLANATION	P.R.	DEBIT	CREDIT	BALANCE
Oct.31					4 0 0 0 00

Stephanie Ross, Withdrawals — Account No. 302

DATE	EXPLANATION	P.R.	DEBIT	CREDIT	BALANCE
Oct. 31					8 0 0 00

Repair Services Revenue — Account No. 403

DATE	EXPLANATION	P.R.	DEBIT	CREDIT	BALANCE
Oct. 31					1 8 0 0 00

Amortization Expense, Office Equipment — Account No. 612

DATE	EXPLANATION	P.R.	DEBIT	CREDIT	BALANCE

Rent Expense — Account No. 640

DATE	EXPLANATION	P.R.	DEBIT	CREDIT	BALANCE

Office Supplies Expense — Account No. 650

DATE	EXPLANATION	P.R.	DEBIT	CREDIT	BALANCE

DATE	ACCOUNT TITLES AND EXPLANATION	P.R.	DEBIT	CREDIT

STEPHANIE ROSS

Income Statement

For Month Ended October 31, 20__

Revenue:				
Repair services revenue				
Operating expenses:				
Amortization expense, office equipment				
Rent expense				
Office supplies expense				
Total operating expenses				
Net income				

STEPHANIE ROSS

Statement of Owner's Equity

For Month Ended October 31, 20__

Stephanie Ross, capital, October 1, 20__				
October net income				
Less withdrawals				
Excess of income over withdrawals				
Stephanie Ross, capital, October 31, 20__				

STEPHANIE ROSS

Balance Sheet

October 31, 20___

Assets										
Cash										
Office supplies										
Prepaid rent										
Office equipment										
Less accumulated amortization										
Total assets										
Liabilities										
Accounts payable										
Owner's Equity										
Stephanie Ross, capital, October 31, 20___										
Total liabilities and owner's equity										

Problem V

a. Long Company has one employee who earns $80.00 per day. The company operates with monthly accounting periods, and the employee is paid each Friday night for a workweek that begins on Monday. Assume the calendar for October appears as shown and enter the four $400.00 weekly wage payments directly in the T-accounts below. Then enter the adjustment for the wages earned but unpaid on October 31.

OCTOBER						
S	M	T	W	T	F	S
	1	2	3	4	5	6
7	8	9	10	11	12	13
14	15	16	17	18	19	20
21	22	23	24	25	26	27
28	29	30	31			

Cash	Wages Payable	Wages Expense

b. Blade Company's October income statement should show $_____ of wages expense, and its October 31 balance sheet should show a $_____ liability for wages payable. The wages earned by its employee but unpaid on October 31 are an example of an _____ expense.

c. In the space that follows give the general journal entry to record payment of a full week's wages to the Blade Company employee on November 2.

GENERAL JOURNAL   Page 1

DATE	ACCOUNT TITLES AND EXPLANATION	P.R.	DEBIT	CREDIT
Nov.2				

Problem VI

Riverview Properties operates an apartment building. On December 31, at the end of an annual accounting period, its Rent Earned account had a $335,500 credit balance, and the Unearned Rent account had a $3,600 credit balance. The following information was available for the year-end adjustments: (a) the credit balance in the Unearned Rent account resulted from a tenant paying his rent for six months in advance beginning on November 1; (b) also, a tenant in temporary financial difficulties had not paid his rent for the month of December. The amount due was $475.

Required: Enter the necessary adjustments directly in the T-accounts below.

Rent Receivable	Unearned Rent	Rent Earned
	Nov. 1 3,600	Balance 335,500

After the foregoing adjustments are entered in the accounts, the company's Rent Earned account has a $_____ balance which should appear on its income statement as revenue earned during the year. Its Unearned Rent account has a $_____ balance, and this should appear on the company's balance sheet as a _____. Likewise, the company's Rent Receivable account has a $_____ balance, and this should appear on its balance sheet as a _____.

Problem VII

Under the cash basis of accounting, revenues are reported as being earned in the accounting period in which _____; expenses are charged to the period in which _____; and net income for the period is the difference between _____ and _____. Under the accrual basis of accounting, revenues are credited to the period in which _____, expenses are _____ with revenues, and no consideration is given as to when cash is received or disbursed.

Problem VIII (This problem applies to Appendix B.)

The following statements are either true or false. Place a (T) in the parentheses before each true statement and an (F) before each false statement.

1.   ( ) If a business follows the practice of debiting prepayments of expenses to expense accounts, the adjusting entries for prepaid expenses require debits to prepaid expense accounts.

2.   ( ) If a business records receipts of unearned revenues with debits to cash and credits to revenue accounts, no adjusting entries are required at the end of the period.

Problem IX (This problem applies to Appendix B.)

You are given several words, phrases, or numbers to choose from in completing each of the following statements or in answering the following questions. In each case select the one that best completes the statement or answers the question and place its letter in the answer space provided.

_____ 1. Richley Company prepares monthly financial statements and follows the procedure of crediting revenue accounts when it records cash receipts of unearned revenues. During April, the business received $4,800 for services to be rendered during April and May. On April 30, $2,000 of the amounts received had been earned. What is the adjusting journal entry on April 30 for service fees?

    a. Service Fees Earned 2,000

          Unearned Service Fees 2,000

    b. Unearned Service Fees 2,800

          Service Fees Earned 2,800

    c. Cash...2,000

          Service Fees Earned... 2,000

    d. Unearned Service Fees 2,000

          Service Fees Earned 2,000

    e. Service Fees Earned 2,800

          Unearned Service Fees 2,800

_____ 2. Xu Company prepares monthly financial statements. On August 31, the balance in the Office Supplies account was $300. During September, $500 of supplies were purchased and debited to Office Supplies Expense. What is the adjusting journal entry on September 30 to adjust for the supplies assuming a September inventory of supplies showed that $250 were on hand.

    a. Office Supplies..350

          Office Supplies Expense.. 350

    b. Office Supplies Expense 250

          Office Supplies 250

    c. Office Supplies Expense 50

          Office Supplies 50

    d. Office Supplies Expense..350

          Office Supplies 350

    e. Office Supplies...250

          Office Supplies Expense 250

Solutions for Chapter 4

Problem I

1. T
2. T
3. F
4. T
5. F

Problem II

1. D
2. C
3. B
4. E
5. D
6. C

Problem III

13	Accounting form balance sheet	12	External transactions
18	Accounting period	2	Intangible assets
1	Accrual basis accounting	19	Interim financial reports
10	Accrued expenses	14	Internal transactions
4	Accrued revenues	8	Market value of an asset
15	Adjusted trial balance	22	Matching principle
21	Adjusting entry	24	Property, plant and equipment
5	Amortization	26	Prepaid expense
25	Book value of an asset	16	Report form balance sheet
7	Capital assets	6	Reporting period
27	Cash basis accounting	28	Straight-line amortization method
20	Contra account	23	Time-period principle
3	Correcting entries	17	Unadjusted trial balance
11	Depreciation	9	Unearned revenues

Problem IV

Oct. 31	Rent Expense		515.00	
	Prepaid Rent			515.00
31	Office Supplies Expense		35.00	
	Office Supplies			35.00
31	Amortization Expense, Office Equipment		35.00	
	Accumulated Depr., Office Equipment			35.00

STEPHANIE ROSS
Worksheet
October 31, 20___

	Unadjusted Trial Balance		Adjustments		Adjusted Trial Balance	
	Dr.	Cr.	Dr.	Cr.	Dr.	Cr.
Cash	2,530				2,530	
Office supplies	75			35	40	
Prepaid rent	1,545			515	1,030	
Office equipment	1,625				1,625	
Accumulated amortization, office equipment				35		35
Accounts payable		775				775
Stephanie Ross, capital		4,000				4,000
Stephanie Ross, withdrawals	800				800	
Repair services revenue		1,800				1,800
Amortization expense, office equipment			35		35	
Rent expense			515		515	
Office supplies expense			35		35	
Totals	$6,575	$6,575	$585	$585	$6,610	$6,610

Cash

Date	Debit	Credit	Balance
Oct 31			2,530.00

Accounts Payable

Date	Debit	Credit	Balance
Oct.31			775.00

Stephanie Ross, Capital

Date	Debit	Credit	Balance
Oct. 31			4,000.00

Office Supplies

Date	Debit	Credit	Balance
Oct. 31			75.00
31		35.00	40.00

Stephanie Ross, Withdrawals

Date	Debit	Credit	Balance
Oct. 31			800.00

Prepaid Rent

Date	Debit	Credit	Balance
Oct. 31			1,545.00
31		515.00	1,030.00

Repair Services Revenue

Date	Debit	Credit	Balance
Oct. 31			1,800.00

Amort. Expense, Office Equipment

Date	Debit	Credit	Balance
Oct. 31	35.00		35.00

Office Equipment

Date	Debit	Credit	Balance
Oct. 31			1,625.00

Rent Expense

Date	Debit	Credit	Balance
Oct. 31	515.00		515.00

Accumulated Amort., Office Equipment

Date	Debit	Credit	Balance
Oct. 31		35.00	35.00

Office Supplies Expense

Date	Debit	Credit	Balance
Oct. 31	35.00		35.00

STEPHANIE ROSS
Income Statement
For Month Ended October 31, 20--

Revenue:		
Repair services revenue		$1,800.00
Operating expenses:		
Amortization expense, office equipment	$ 35.00	
Rent expense	515.00	
Office supplies expense	35.00	
Total operating expenses		585.00
Net income		$1,215.00

STEPHANIE ROSS
Statement of Owner's Equity
For Month Ended October 31, 20--

Stephanie Ross, capital, October 1, 20--		$4,000.00
October net income	$1,215.00	
Less withdrawals	800.00	
Excess of income over withdrawals		415.00
Stephanie Ross, capital, October 31, 20--		$4,415.00

STEPHANIE ROSS
Balance Sheet
October 31, 20--
Assets

Cash		$2,530.00
Office supplies		40.00
Prepaid rent		1,030.00
Office equipment	$1,625.00	
Less accumulated amortization	35.00	1,590.00
Total assets		$5,190.00
Liabilities		
Accounts payable		$775.00
Owner's Equity		
Stephanie Ross, Capital, October 31, 20--		4,415.00
Total liabilities and owner's equity		$5,190.00

Problem V

a.

Cash					Wages Expense		
	Oct. 5	400.00		Oct. 5	400.00		
	12	400.00		12	400.00		
	19	400.00		19	400.00		
	26	400.00		26	400.00		
				31	240.00		

Wages Payable		
	Oct. 31	240.00

b. $1,840.00; $240.00; accrued

c. Nov 2   Wages Expense 160.00

   Wages Payable 240.00

   Cash 400.00

Problem VI

Rent Receivable				Unearned Rent			
Dec. 31	475			Dec. 31	1,200	Nov. 1	3,600
							2,400

Rent Earned		
	Bal.	335,500
	Dec. 31	1,200
	31	475
		337,175

Rent Earned, $337,175

Unearned Rent, $2,400, liability

Rent Receivable, $475, asset

Problem VII

they are received in cash, they are paid, revenue receipts, expense disbursements, they are earned, matched

Problem VIII

1. T
2. F

Problem IX

1. E
2. C

Learning Objective 1:

Describe and prepare a work sheet and explain its usefulness.

Summary

A work sheet is optional and can be a useful tool in preparing and analyzing financial statements. It is helpful at the end of a period for preparing adjusting entries, an adjusted trial balance, and financial statements. A work sheet often contains five pairs of columns for an unadjusted trial balance, the adjustments, an adjusted trial balance, an income statement, and the balance sheet (including the statement of owner's equity).

Learning Objective 2:

Describe the closing process and explain why temporary accounts are closed each period.

Summary

The closing process is the final step of the accounting cycle; it closes temporary accounts at the end of each accounting period: (1) to update the owner's capital account for revenue, expense, and withdrawals transactions recorded for the period; and (2) to prepare revenue, expense and withdrawals accounts for the next reporting period by giving them zero balances.

Learning Objective 3:

Prepare closing entries.

Summary

Closing entries involve four steps: (1) close credit balances in revenue accounts to Income Summary, (2) close debit balances in expense accounts to Income Summary, (3) close Income Summary to owner's capital, and (4) close withdrawals account to owner's capital.

Learning Objective 4:

Explain and prepare a post-closing trial balance.

Summary

A post-closing trial balance is a list of permanent accounts and their balances after all closing entries are journalized and posted. Permanent accounts are asset, liability and owner's equity accounts. The purpose of a post-closing trial balance is to verify that (1) total debits equal total credits for permanent accounts and (2) all temporary accounts have zero balances.

Learning Objective 5:

Describe the steps in the accounting cycle.

Summary

The accounting cycle consists of nine steps: (1) analyze transactions, (2) journalize, (3) post, (4) prepare unadjusted trial balance, (5) adjust, (6) prepare adjusted trial balance, (7) prepare statements, (8) close, (9) prepare post-closing trial balance. If a work sheet is prepared, it covers Steps 4 to 6. Reversing entries is an optional step that is done between steps 9 and 1.

Learning Objective 6:

Explain and prepare a classified balance sheet.

Summary

Classified balance sheets usually report four groups of assets: current assets; long-term investments; property, plant, and equipment; and intangible assets. Also, they include at least two groups of liabilities: current and long-term. Owner's equity for proprietorships reports the capital account balance.

Learning Objective 7 (Appendix 5A):

Prepare reversing entries and explain their purpose.

Summary

Reversing entries are an optional step. They are applied to accrued assets and liabilities. The purpose of reversing entries is to simplify subsequent journal entries. Financial statements are unaffected by the choice to use reversing entries or not.

Learning Objective 8 (Appendix 5B):

Compute the current ratio and describe what it reveals about a company's financial condition.

Summary

A company's current ratio is defined as current assets divided by current liabilities. We use it to evaluate a company's ability to pay its current liabilities out of current assets.

I. **Work Sheet as a Tool**—informal document that gathers information about the accounts, the needed adjustments, and the financial statements. The informal documents are called *working papers*.

   A. Benefits: useful in preparing interim financial statements, captures linked accounting information, helps organize an audit, helps avoid errors.

   B. Work Sheet: has five sets of double columns; steps to prepare:

   1. Enter unadjusted trial balance in the first two columns.

   2. Enter adjustments in the third and fourth columns. Total columns to verify debit adjustments equal credit adjustments. These adjusting entries must also be entered in the journal and posted to the ledger.

   3. Prepare adjusted trial balance by combining the adjustments with the unadjusted balances for each account. Total Adjusted Trial Balance columns confirm debits equal credits.

   4. Extend adjusted trial balance amounts to financial statement columns.

   5. Enter net income (or loss) and balance the financial statement columns.

   6. Prepare financial statements from work sheet information.

II. **Closing Process**—an important step to prepare accounts for recording the transactions of the next period. Closing is performed at the end of an accounting period after financial statements are prepared.

   A. In the closing process we must:

   1. Identify accounts for closing.

   2. Record and post closing entries.

   3. Prepare a post-closing trial balance.

   B. Closing entries are a necessary step because we want the:

   1. Revenue, expense, and withdrawals accounts to begin with zero balances to measure the results from the period just ending.

   2. Owner's capital account to reflect (a) increases from net income and (b) decreases from net losses and withdrawals from the period just ending.

   C. Temporary and Permanent Accounts

   1. Temporary (or nominal) accounts accumulate data related to one accounting period. These include all income statement accounts, withdrawals accounts, and the Income Summary.

   2. Permanent (or real) accounts report on activities related to one or more future accounting periods. They carry their ending balances into the next period. These include all balance sheet accounts.

   3. The closing process applies only to temporary accounts.

Chapter Outline

Notes

III.   Recording and Posting Closing Entries

      1. Closing entries transfer the end-of-period balances in the revenue, expense, and withdrawals to the permanent owner's capital account. The four closing entries are:

         a. Transfer revenue account balances to Income Summary.

         b. Transfer expense account balances to Income Summary.

         c. Close Income Summary to owner's capital account. The balance of Income Summary represents net income or net loss.

         d. Close withdrawals account balances to the owner's capital account.

IV.   Post-Closing Trial Balance

      1. Lists permanent accounts and their balances: includes assets, liabilities, and owner's capital.

      2. Prepared after all closing entries are journalized and posted.

      3. Verifies that total debits equal total credits for permanent accounts, and all temporary accounts have zero balances.

V.   Reviewing the Accounting Cycle—the sequence of accounting procedures followed each accounting period:

    A. Analyze transactions

    B. Journalize

    C. Post

    D. Unadjusted trial balance

    E. Adjust

    F. Adjusted trial balance

    G. Prepare statements

    H. Close

    I. Post-closing trial balance

IV.   Classified Balance Sheet—organizes assets and liabilities into sub-groups:

    A. Current assets—cash and other resources that are expected to be sold, collected, or used within the longer of one year or the company's operating cycle; includes cash, temporary investments in marketable securities, accounts receivable, notes receivable, goods for sale to customers (merchandise inventory), prepaid expenses.

B. Long-term investments—held for more than one year or the operating cycle; includes long-term notes receivable, investments in share and bonds, and often includes land not being used in operations.

C. Property, plant and equipment (PPE) —known as fixed assets, tangible capital assets used to produce or sell products and services for more than one accounting period; equipment, vehicles, buildings, land.

D. Intangible assets—Long-term resources used to produce or sell products and services; lack physical form and benefits are uncertain; their value comes from the privileges or rights granted to or held by the owner; copyrights, franchises, trademarks, goodwill.

E. Current liabilities—obligations due to be paid or settled within one year or the operating cycle; usually settled by paying out current assets; accounts payable, notes payable, wages payable, taxes payable, interest payable, unearned revenues, current portion of long-term liability.

F. Long-term liabilities—obligations that are not due within one year or the operating cycle of the business; notes payable, mortgages payable, bonds payable, lease obligations.

G. Owner's equity—the owner's claim on the assets of a company. Reported in the equity section as owner's capital for a proprietorship, partner's capital for a partnership, and shareholders' equity for a corporation.

VII. **Appendix 5A: Reversing Entries and Account Numbering**

Reversing entries: optional entries prepared on the first day of the new accounting period; prepared for those adjusting entries that created accrued assets and liabilities.

VIII. **Appendix 5B: Using the Information**

Current ratio:

1. Current assets divided by current liabilities
2. Measures a company's ability to pay its short-term obligations
3. Liquidity: the ability to pay day-to-day obligations with existing liquid assets.
4. Liquid assets: those that can be easily converted to cash or used to pay for services or obligations. Cash is the most liquid asset.

THE ACCOUNTING CYCLE
This Cycle Assumes a Work Sheet is Used

STEPS	PURPOSE	TIMING
1. Analyze transaction	In preparation for journalizing	During the period
2. Journalize	Record debits and credits in a journal	During the period
3. Post	Transfer debits and credits from journal entries to the ledger accounts	During the period
4. Work sheet	• Unadjusted trial balance columns: summarize ledger accounts and amounts • Adjusting columns: record adjustments to bring account balances up to date; journalize and post adjusting entries to the accounts • Adjusted trial balance columns: Summarize adjusted ledger accounts and amounts	End of period
5. Prepare statements	Use adjusted trial balance to prepare statements	End of period
6. Close	Journalize and post entries to close temporary accounts and update the owner's capital account.	End of period
7. Post-closing trial balance	Test clerical accuracy of adjusting and closing steps.	End of period

VISUAL #8

MUSIC COMPONENTS
BALANCE SHEET
JANUARY 31, 2005

Assets
Current assets:

Cash	$ 6,500	
Temporary investments	2,100	
Accounts receivable	4,400	
Notes receivable	1,500	
Merchandise inventory	27,500	
Prepaid expenses	2,400	
Total current assets		$ 44,400

Long-term investments:

Notes receivable, due March 31, 2007	18,000	
Land not currently used in operations	48,000	
Total investments		66,000

Property, plant and equipment:

Land		73,200	
Buildings	$170,000		
Less: Accumulated amortization	45,000	125,000	
Store equipment	$ 33,200		
Less Accumulated Amortization	8,000	25,200	
Total property, plant, and equipment			223,400

Intangible assets:

Trademark	10,000
Total Assets	$343,800

Liabilities
Current liabilities:

Accounts Payable	$ 15,300	
Wages Payable	3,200	
Notes Payable	3,000	
Current portion of long-term liabilities	7,500	
Total current liabilities		$ 29,000

Long-term liabilities:

Notes payable (less current portion)	150,000	
Total liabilities		$179,000

Owner's equity

Donald Bowie, capital	164,800
Total liabilities and owner's equity	$343,800

Problem I

The following statements are either true or false. Place a (T) in the parentheses before each true statement and an (F) before each false statement.

1. ( ) Throughout the current period, one could refer to the balance of the Income Summary account to determine the amount of net income or loss that was earned in the prior accounting period.

2. ( ) The only reason why the Statement of Owner's Equity or Balance Sheet columns of a work sheet might be out of balance would be if an error had been made in sorting revenue and expense data from the Adjusted Trial Balance columns of the work sheet.

3. ( ) If the Income Statement columns of a work sheet are equal after transferring from the Adjusted Trial Balance columns, then it can be concluded that there is no net income (or loss).

4. ( ) The value of intangible assets comes from the privileges or rights granted to or held by the owner.

5. ( ) After all closing entries are posted at the end of an accounting period, the Income Summary account balance is zero.

Problem II

You are given several words, phrases, or numbers to choose from in completing each of the following statements or in answering the following question. In each case select the one that best completes the statement or answers the question and place its letter in the answer space provided.

_____ 1. Inventory, Rent Expense, and The Owner, Capital would be sorted to which respective columns in completing a work sheet?

a. Statement of Owner's Equity or Balance Sheet—Debit; Income Statement—Debit; and Statement of Owner's Equity or Balance Sheet—Debit.

b. Statement of Owner's Equity or Balance Sheet—Debit; Income Statement—Debit; and Statement of Owner's Equity or Balance Sheet—Credit.

c. Statement of Owner's Equity or Balance Sheet—Debit; Income Statement— Credit; and Statement of Owner's Equity or Balance Sheet—Debit.

d. Statement of Owner's Equity or Balance Sheet—Debit; Income Statement— Credit; and Statement of Owner's Equity or Balance Sheet—Credit.

e. Statement of Owner's Equity or Balance Sheet—Credit; Income Statement— Credit; and Statement of Owner's Equity or Balance Sheet—Credit.

2. Based on the following T-accounts and their end-of-period balances, what will be the balance of the Bill Atkins, Capital account after the closing entries are posted?

Bill Atkins, Capital		
	Dec. 31	7,000

Bill Atkins, Withdrawals		
Dec. 31	9,600	

Income Summary

Revenue		
	Dec. 31	29,700

Rent Expense		
Dec. 31	3,600	

Salaries Expense		
Dec. 31	7,200	

Insurance Expense		
Dec. 31	920	

Amort. Expense, Equipment		
Dec. 31	500	

Accum. Amort. Equipment		
	Dec.31	500

a. $12,880 Debit.
b. $12,880 Credit.
c. $24,480 Credit.
d. $14,880 Credit.
e. $10,480 Debit.

3. The following items appeared on a December 31 work sheet. Based on the following information, what are the totals in the Statement of Owner's Equity or Balance Sheet columns?

	Unadjusted Trial Balance		Adjustments	
	Debit	Credit	Debit	Credit
Cash	975			
Supplies	180			70
Prepaid insurance	3,600			150
Equipment	10,320			
Accounts payable		1,140		
Unearned fees		4,500	375	
The Owner, capital		9,180		
The Owner, withdrawals	1,650			
Fees earned		5,850		375
				300
Salaries expense	2,100		315	
Rent expense	1,500			
Utilities expense	345			
	20,670	20,670		
Insurance expense			150	
Supplies expense			70	
Amortization expense, equipment			190	
Accumulated amortization, equipment				190
Salaries payable				315
Accounts receivable			300	
			1,400	1,400

a. $16,805.
b. $16,505.
c. $14,950.
d. $14,820.
e. Some other amount.

_____ 4. On a classified balance sheet, current assets include:

a. Cash, Accounts payable, Inventory, and Equipment.

b. Wages payable, Cash, Accounts receivable, and Temporary investments.

c. Prepaid expenses, Accounts receivable, Inventory, and Cash.

d. Land, Accounts payable, Prepaid expenses, and Inventory.

e. Temporary investments, Accounts receivable, Prepaid expenses, and Accumulated Amortization.

_____ 5. Temporary accounts are:

a. Accounts that are not closed at the end of the accounting period; therefore, assets, liabilities and equity accounts.

b. Accounts used to record the owner's investment in the business plus any more or less permanent changes in the owner's equity.

c. Accounts the balance of which is subtracted from the balance of an associated account to show a more proper amount for the item recorded in the associated account.

d. Also called nominal accounts.

e. Also called real accounts.

_____ 6. The following information is available from the financial statements of Platinum Company:

Current assets	$ 195,000
Current liabilities	113,500
Total liabilities	441,500
Intangible assets	20,000
Property, plant, and equipment	575,000
Shareholder's equity	408,500

The amount of long-term investments showing on the balance sheet is:

a. $381,500

b. $81,500

c. $226,500

d. $80,000

e. $60,000

Problem III

Many of the important ideas and concepts discussed in Chapter 5 are reflected in the following list of key terms. Test your understanding of these terms by matching the appropriate definitions with the terms. Record the number identifying the most appropriate definition in the blank space next to each term.

	Capital assets		Long-term liabilities
	Classified balance sheet		Operating cycle
	Closing entries		Owner's equity
	Closing process		Permanent accounts
	Current assets		Post-closing trial balance
	Current ratio		Pro forma statements
	Current liabilities		Property, plant and equipment
	Income summary		Reversing entries
	Intangible assets		Temporary accounts
	Intangible capital assets		Unclassified balance sheet
	Liquidity		Work sheet
	Liquid assets		Working papers
	Long-term investments		

1.   A list of permanent accounts and their balances from the ledger after all closing entries are journalized and posted; a list of balances for all accounts not closed.

2.   A ratio that is used to evaluate a company's ability to pay its short-term obligations, calculated by dividing current assets by current liabilities.

3.   Optional entries recorded at the beginning of a new period that prepare the accounts for simplified journal entries subsequent to accrual adjusting entries.

4.   Long-lived capital assets that lack physical form and are used to produce or sell products or services. Goodwill is an intangible asset but it is not a capital asset.

5.   The owner's claim on the assets of a company.

6.   Journal entries recorded at the end of each accounting period that transfers the end-of-period balances in revenue, expense, and withdrawals accounts to the permanent owner's capital account in order to prepare for the upcoming period and update the owner's capital account for the events of the period just finished.

7.   A balance sheet that broadly groups the assets, liabilities, and owner's equity.

8.   Internal documents that are used to assist the preparers in doing the analyses and organizing the information for reports to be presented to internal and external decision makers.

9.   Assets not used in day-to-day operating activities that are held for more than one year or the operating cycle such as a long-term note receivable.

10.   Accounts that are used to report on activities related to one or more future accounting periods; their balances are carried into the next period, and include all balance sheet accounts; permanent account balances are not closed as long as the company continues to own the assets, owe the liabilities, and have owner's equity; also called real accounts.

11. A step at the end of the accounting period that prepares accounts for recording the transactions of the next period.

12. Accounts that are used to describe revenues, expenses, and owner's withdrawals for one accounting period; they are closed at the end of the reporting period; also called nominal accounts.

13. Long-lived capital tangible capital assets used to produce or sell products and services; abbreviated PPE and sometimes called fixed assets.

14. Long-term assets (resources) used to produce or sell products or services; these assets lack physical form.

15. Assets that can be easily converted to cash or used to pay for services or obligations; cash is the most liquid asset.

16. Long-lived assets used to produce or sell products and services and consist of tangible assets called property, plant and equipment, and intangible capital assets.

17. Obligations that are not due to be paid within the longer of one year or the operating cycle.

18. Cash or other assets that are expected to be sold, collected, or used within the longer of one year or the company's operating cycle.

19. For a business, the average time between paying cash for employee salaries or merchandise and rece4iving cash from customers.

20. Statements that show the effects of the proposed transactions as if the transactions had already occurred.

21. A temporary account used only in the closing process to which t6he balances of revenue and expense accounts are transferred; its balance equals net income or net loss and is transferred to the owner's capital account.

22. A balance sheet that presents the assets and liabilities in relevant subgroups.

23. Obligations due to be paid or settled within the longer of one year or the operating cycle.

24. The ability to pay day-to-day obligations (current liabilities) with existing liquid assets.

Problem IV

Complete the following by filling in the blanks.

1. A work sheet is prepared after all transactions are recorded but before _____.

2. Revenue accounts have credit balances; consequently, to close a revenue account and make it show a zero balance, the revenue account is _____ and the Income Summary account is _____ for the amount of the balance.

3. In extending the amounts in the Adjusted Trial Balance columns of a work sheet to the proper Income Statement or Statement of Changes in Owner's Equity and Balance Sheet columns, two decisions are required:
   (a)_____and
   (b)_____.

4. Expense accounts have debit balances; therefore, expense accounts are_____ and the Income Summary account is _____ in closing the expense accounts.

5. In preparing a work sheet for a business, its unadjusted account balances are entered in the _____ columns of the work sheet form, after which the _____ are entered in the second pair of columns. Next, the unadjusted trial balance amounts and the amounts in the Adjustments columns are combined to secure an _____ in the third pair of columns.

6. Only balance sheet accounts should have balances appearing on the post-closing trial balance because the balances of all temporary accounts are reduced to _____ in the closing procedure.

7. Closing entries are necessary because if at the end of an accounting period the revenue and expense accounts are to show only one period's revenues and expenses, they must begin the period with _____ balances, and closing entries cause the revenue and expense accounts to begin a new period with _____ balances.

8. Closing entries accomplish two purposes: (1) they cause all _____ accounts to begin the new accounting period with zero balances, and (2) they transfer the net effect of the past period's _____, _____, and withdrawal transactions to the owner's capital account.

Problem V

The unfinished year-end work sheet of Jason's Home Shop appears on the next page.

Required:

1. Complete the work sheet using the following adjustments information:

   a. Inventory of shop supplies indicates that $725 of shop supplies remained on hand.

   b. Amortization of shop equipment was $475 during the year.

   c. On December 31, wages of $388 have been earned by the one employee but are unpaid because payment is not due.

2. After completing the work sheet, prepare the year-end adjusting and closing entries.

3. Post the adjusting and closing entries to the accounts that are provided in the abbreviated general ledger.

4. After posting the adjusting and closing entries, prepare a post-closing trial balance.

JASON'S HOME SHOP
Work Sheet For the Year Ended December 31, 2005

ACCOUNT	UNADJUSTED TRIAL BALANCE DR.	UNADJUSTED TRIAL BALANCE CR.	ADJUSTMENTS DR.	ADJUSTMENTS CR.	ADJUSTED TRIAL BALANCE DR.	ADJUSTED TRIAL BALANCE CR.	INCOME STATEMENT DR.	INCOME STATEMENT CR.	STMT. OF O.E. AND BALANCE SHEET DR.	STMT. OF O.E. AND BALANCE SHEET CR.
Cash	2 8 7 5 00									
Accounts receivable	2 0 0 0 00									
Shop supplies	1 7 6 2 00									
Shop equipment	5 1 2 5 00									
Accumulated amortization, shop equipment		7 2 5 00								
Accounts payable		5 7 5 00								
Jason Painter, capital		5 5 0 0 00								
Jason Painter, Withdrawals	30 0 0 0 00									
Repair services Revenue		55 7 8 5 00								
Wages expense	18 2 5 0 00									
Rent expense	2 5 0 0 00									
Miscellaneous Expenses	7 3 00									
	62 5 8 5 00	62 5 8 5 00								
Shop supplies Expense										
Amortization expense, shop Equipment										
Wages payable										

Fundamental Accounting Principles, 11th Canadian Edition

GENERAL JOURNAL

Page 1

DATE	ACCOUNT TITLES AND EXPLANATION	P.R.	DEBIT	CREDIT

GENERAL LEDGER

Cash

Date	Debit	Credit	Balance
Dec. 31			2,875.00

Jason Painter, Withdrawals

Date	Debit	Credit	Balance
Dec. 31			30,000.00

Accounts Receivable

Date	Debit	Credit	Balance
Dec. 31			2,000.00

Repair Services Revenue

Date	Debit	Credit	Balance
Dec. 31			55,785.00

Shop Supplies

Date	Debit	Credit	Balance
Dec. 31			1,762.00

Amort. Expense, Shop Equipment

Date	Debit	Credit	Balance

Shop Equipment

Date	Debit	Credit	Balance
Dec. 31			5,125.00

Wages Expense

Date	Debit	Credit	Balance
Dec. 31			18,250.00

Accum. Amort., Shop Equipment

Date	Debit	Credit	Balance
Dec. 31			725.00

Rent Expense

Date	Debit	Credit	Balance
Dec. 31			2,500.00

Accounts Payable

Date	Debit	Credit	Balance
Dec. 31			575.00

Shop Supplies Expense

Date	Debit	Credit	Balance

Wages Payable

Date	Debit	Credit	Balance

Office Expenses

Date	Debit	Credit	Balance
Dec. 31			73.00

Jason Painter, Capital

Date	Debit	Credit	Balance
Dec. 31			5,500.00

Income Summary

Date	Debit	Credit	Balance

JASON'S HOME SHOP

Post-Closing Trial Balance

December 31, 2005

Cash						
Accounts receivable						
Shop supplies						
Shop equipment						
Accumulated amortization, shop equipment						
Accounts payable						
Wages payable						
Jason Painter, capital						
Totals						

Problem VI

The following accounts and their balances were reported for Chang's Novelty Store at November 30, 2005, their fiscal year end.

Required: Classify these accounts as on a classified balance sheet and answer the following questions.

1. What is the amount of total current assets?

2. What is the amount of total long-term investments?

3. What is the amount of total property, plant, and equipment?

4. What is the amount of total intangible assets?

5. What is the amount of total assets?

6. What is the amount of total current liabilities?

7. What is the amount of total long-term liabilities?

8. What is the amount of owner's equity?

9. What is the amount of total liabilities and owner's equity?

	Trial Balance	
	Debit	Credit
Accounts payable		$4,000
Accounts receivable	$12,800	
Accumulated amortization, equipment		6,000
Cash	5,000	
Copyright	7,000	
Equipment	23,000	
Land not currently used in operations	54,000	
Land (used in operations)	67,000	
Note payable (including current portion of $6,000)		92,000
Notes receivable, due in 3 years	15,000	
Prepaid insurance	2,400	
Salaries payable		1,300
Supplies	600	
Trademark	8,000	
Y. Chang, capital		101,500
Y. Chang, withdrawals	10,000	
	204,800	204,800

Problem VII (This problem applies to Appendix 5A.)

You are given several words, phrases, or numbers to choose from in completing each of the following statements or in answering the following questions. In each case select the one that best completes the statement or answers the question and place its letter in the answer space provided.

_____ 1. The December 31,2005, adjusting entries for Mary Loretti's interior design company included accrual of $760 in assistant salaries. This amount will be paid on January 10, as part of the normal $1,200 salary for two weeks. The bookkeeper for the company uses reversing entries where appropriate. The entry to record the payment of the assistant's salary January 10,2006, was:

Jan. 10	Salaries Expense..	1,200
	Cash...	1,200

What was the January 1, 2006, reversing entry?

a.	Salaries Payable	760	
	Salaries Expense..	440	
	Cash		1,200
b.	Salaries Payable	440	
	Salaries Expense		440
c.	Salaries Payable	760	
	Salaries Expense		760
d.	Cash..	1,200	
	Salaries Expense..		1,200
e.	The bookkeeper would not make a reversing entry for this transaction.		

_____ 2. On December 31, 2005, K Company accrued salaries expense with an adjusting entry. No reversing entry was made and the payment of the salaries during January 2006 was correctly recorded. If X Company had recorded an entry on January 1, 2006, to reverse the accrual, and the subsequent payment was correctly recorded, the effect on the 2006 financial statements of using the reversing entry would have been:

a. to increase net income and reduce liabilities.

b. to increase 2006 expense and reduce assets.

c. to decrease 2006 expense and increase liabilities.

d. to decrease 2006 expense and decrease liabilities.

e. No effect.

Problem VIII (This problem applies to Appendix 5B.)

The following statements are either true or false. Place a (T) in the parentheses before each true statement and an (F) before each false statement.

1. ( ) The current ratio, calculated by dividing the amount current assets by the amount current liabilities, is used to evaluate a company's ability to pay its short-term obligations.

2. ( ) Liquidity refers to the ability to pay day-to-day assets with current liabilities.

Solutions for Chapter 5

Problem I

1. F
2. F
3. T
4. T
5. T

Problem II

1. B
2. D
3. A
4. C
5. D
6. E

Problem III

16	Capital assets	17	Long-term liabilities
22	Classified balance sheet	19	Operating cycle
6	Closing entries	5	Owner's equity
11	Closing process	10	Permanent accounts
18	Current assets	1	Post-closing trial balance
2	Current ratio	20	Pro forma statements
23	Current liabilities	13	Property, plant and equipment
21	Income summary	3	Reversing entries
14	Intangible assets	12	Temporary accounts
4	Intangible capital assets	7	Unclassified balance sheet
24	Liquidity	25	Work sheet
15	Liquid assets	8	Working papers
9	Long-term investments		

Problem IV

1. the adjustments are entered in the accounts

2. debited, credited

3. (a) Is the item a debit or a credit?

   (b) On which statement does it appear?

4. credited, debited

5. Unadjusted Trial Balance; adjustments; adjusted trial balance

6. zero

7. zero, zero

8. temporary or nominal, revenue, expense

Problem V

JASON'S HOME SHOP
Work Sheet for Year Ended December 31, 2005

	Unadjusted Trial Balance Dr.	Cr.	Adjustments Dr.	Cr.	Adjusted Trial Balance Dr.	Cr.	Income Statement Dr.	Cr.	Statement of O.E. and Balance Sheet Dr.	Cr.
Cash	2,875				2,875				2,875	
Accounts receivable	2,000				2,000				2,000	
Shop supplies	1,762			(a)1,037	725				725	
Shop equipment	5,125				5,125				5,125	
Accum. amort., shop equipment		725		(b) 475		1,200				1,200
Accounts payable		575				575				575
Jason Painter, capital		5,500				5,500				5,500
Jason Painter, withdrawals	30,000				30,000				30,000	
Repair services revenue		55,785				55,785		55,785		
Wages expense	18,250		(c) 388		18,638		18,638			
Rent expense	2,500				2,500		2,500			
Miscellaneous expenses	73				73		73			
	62,585	62,585								
Shop supplies expense			(a)1037		1,037		1,037			
Amortization expense, shop equipment			(b) 475		475		475			
Wages payable				(c) 388		388				388
			1,900	1,900	63,448	63,448	22,723	55,785	40,725	7,663
Net income							33,062			33,062
							55,785	55,785	40,725	40,725

Dec. 31 Shop Supplies Expense........... 1,037
        Shop Supplies.......................... 1,037

    31 Amort. Expense, Shop Equipment...... 475
        Accumulated Amort., Shop Equipment..... 475

    31 Wages Expense............... 388
        Wages Payable....................... 388

    31 Repair Services Revenue........ 55,785
        Income Summary................... 55,785

    31 Income Summary............... 22,723
        Rent Expense..................... 2,500
        Wages Expense................... 18,638
        Miscellaneous Expenses............... 73
        Shop Supplies Expense............. 1,037
        Amort. Expense, Shop Equipment....... 475

    31 Income Summary............. 33,062
        Jason Painter, Capital............. 33,062

    31 Jason Painter, Capital............. 30,000
        Jason Painter, Withdrawals.............. 30,000

Fundamental Accounting Principles, 11th Canadian Edition

GENERAL LEDGER

Cash

Date	Debit	Credit	Balance
Dec. 31			2,875.00

Accounts Receivable

Date	Debit	Credit	Balance
Dec. 31			2,000.00

Shop Supplies

Date	Debit	Credit	Balance
Dec. 31			1,762.00
31		1,037.00	725.00

Shop Equipment

Date	Debit	Credit	Balance
Dec. 31			5,125.00

Accum. Amort., Shop Equipment

Date	Debit	Credit	Balance
Dec. 31			725.00
31		475.00	1,200.00

Accounts Payable

Date	Debit	Credit	Balance
Dec. 31			575.00

Wages Payable

Date	Debit	Credit	Balance
Dec. 31		388.00	388.00

Jason Painter, Capital

Date	Debit	Credit	Balance
Dec. 31			5,500.00
31		33,062.00	38,562.00
31	30,000.00		8,562.00

Jason Painter, Withdrawals

Date	Debit	Credit	Balance
Dec. 31			30,000.00
31		30,000.00	-0-

Repair Services Revenue

Date	Debit	Credit	Balance
Dec. 31			55,785.00
31	55,785.00		-0-

Amort. Expense, Shop Equipment

Date	Debit	Credit	Balance
Dec. 31	475.00		475.00
31		475.00	-0-

Wages Expense

Date	Debit	Credit	Balance
Dec. 31			18,250.00
31	388.00		18,638.00
31		18,638.00	-0-

Rent Expense

Date	Debit	Credit	Balance
Dec. 31			2,500.00
31		2,500.00	-0-

Shop Supplies Expense

Date	Debit	Credit	Balance
Dec. 31	1,037.00		1,037.00
31		1,037.00	-0-

Office Expenses

Date	Debit	Credit	Balance
Dec. 31			73.00
31		73.00	-0-

Income Summary

Date	Debit	Credit	Balance
Dec. 31		55,785.00	55,785.00
31	22,723.00		33,062.00
31	33,062.00		-0-

JASON'S HOME SHOP
Post-Closing Trial Balance
December 31, 2005

Cash..	$2,875	
Accounts receivable	2,000	
Shop supplies	725	
Shop equipment..	5,125	
Accumulated amortization, shop equipment........................		$1,200
Accounts payable		575
Wages payable		388
Jason Painter, capital...		8,562
	$10,725	$10,725

Problem VI

1. $20,800
2. $69,000
3. $84,000
4. $15,000
5. $188,800
6. $11,300
7. $86,000
8. $91,500
9. $188,800

Problem VII

1. T
2. F

Problem VIII

1. T
2. F

CHAPTER 6
ACCOUNTING FOR MERCHANDISING ACTIVITIES

Learning Objective 1:

Describe merchandising activities and identify business examples.

Summary

Operations of merchandising companies involve buying products and reselling them.

Learning Objective 2:

Identify and explain the important components of income for a merchandising company.

Summary

A merchandiser's costs on an income statement include an amount for cost of goods sold. Gross profit, or gross margin, equals net sales minus cost of goods sold.

Learning Objective 3:

Identify and explain the inventory asset of a merchandising company.

Summary

The current asset section of a merchandising company's balance sheet includes merchandise inventory. Merchandise inventory refers to the products a merchandiser sells and are on hand at the balance sheet date.

Learning Objective 4:

Describe both periodic and perpetual inventory systems.

Summary

A perpetual inventory system continuously tracks the cost of goods on hand and the cost of goods sold. A periodic system accumulates the cost of goods purchased during the period and does not compute the amount of inventory on hand or the cost of goods sold until the end of a period.

Learning Objective 5:

Analyze and record transactions for merchandise purchases using a perpetual system.

Summary

For a perpetual inventory system, purchases net of trade discounts are added (debited) to the Merchandise Inventory account. Purchase discounts and purchase returns and allowances are subtracted (credited) from Merchandise Inventory, and transportation-in costs are added (debited) to Merchandise Inventory.

Learning Objective 6:

Analyze and record transactions for sales of merchandise using a perpetual system.

Summary

A merchandiser records sales at list price less any trade discounts. The cost of items sold is transferred from Merchandise Inventory to Cost of Goods Sold. Refunds or credits given to customers for unsatisfactory merchandise are recorded (debited) in Sales Returns and Allowances, a contra account to Sales. If merchandise is returned and restored to inventory, the cost of this merchandise is removed from Cost of Goods Sold and transferred back to Merchandise Inventory. When cash discounts from the sales price are offered and customers pay within the discount period, the seller records (debits) discounts in Sales Discounts, a contra account to Sales. Debit and credit memoranda are documents sent between buyers and sellers to communicate that the sender is either debiting or crediting an account of the recipient.

Learning Objective 7:

Prepare adjustments for a merchandising company.

Summary

With a perpetual inventory system, it is often required to make an adjustment for inventory shrinkage. This is computed by comparing a physical count of inventory with the Merchandise Inventory account balance. Shrinkage is normally charged to Cost of Goods Sold.

Learning Objective 8:

Define, prepare, and use merchandising income statements.

Summary

Multiple-step income statements include greater detail for sales and expenses than do single-step income statements. Classified multiple-step income statements are usually limited to internal use and show the computation of net sales, and report expenses in categories such as selling and general and administrative. Income statements published for external parties can be either multiple-step or single-step. The gross profit ratio is computed as gross profit divided by net sales. It is an indicator of a company's profitability before deducting operating expenses. A gross profit ratio must be large enough to cover operating expenses and give an adequate net income.

Learning Objective 9:

Prepare closing entries for a merchandising company.

Summary

Temporary accounts of merchandising companies include Sales, Sales Discounts, Sales Returns and Allowances, and Cost of Goods Sold. Each is closed to Income Summary.

Learning Objective 10 (Appendix 6A):

Record and compare merchandising transactions using both periodic and perpetual inventory systems.

Summary

Transactions involving the sale and purchase of merchandise are recorded and analyzed under both inventory systems. Adjusting and closing entries for both inventory systems are also illustrated and explained.

Learning Objective 11 (Appendix 6B):

Explain and record Provincial Sales Tax (PST) and Goods and Services Tax (GST).

Summary

PST is a consumption tax applied on sales to final consumers that varies in percent between provinces. GST is a 7% tax collected on most sales but full credit is received for GST paid.

I.   **Merchandising Activities**

    1. A merchandiser earns net income by buying and selling merchandise.

    2. Merchandise consists of products (goods) that a company acquires for the purpose of reselling them to customers.

    3. The cost of these goods is an expense called cost of goods sold.

II.   **Reporting Financial Performance**—revenue (*net sales*) from selling merchandise minus *cost of goods sold* results in *gross profit (gross margin)*. This amount minus *operating expenses* determines the net income or loss for the period.

III. **Reporting Financial Position**

A. Merchandise Inventory

    1. A merchandising company's balance sheet includes one additional *current* asset called *Merchandise Inventory*: products a company owns for the purpose of selling to customers.

    2. The cost of this asset includes the cost incurred to buy the goods, ship them to the store, and other costs necessary to make them ready for sale.

B.   Operating Cycle—begins with the purchase of merchandise and ends with the collection of cash from the sale of merchandise.

IV.   Inventory Systems—two systems used to collect information about *cost of goods sold* and cost of inventory on hand.

    1. *Perpetual inventory system*—gives a continual record of the amount of inventory on hand. Accumulates the net cost of merchandise purchases in the inventory account and transfers the cost of each sale from the same inventory account to cost of goods sold when an item is sold; provides up-to-date cost of goods sold.

    2. *Periodic inventory systems*—requires updating the inventory account only at the end of a period to reflect the quantity and cost of both goods on hand and goods sold; does not require continual updating of the inventory account; records the cost of new merchandise in a temporary expense account called *Purchases*.

Note: Transactions involving a periodic inventory system are contained in Appendix 6A.

Chapter Outline

V. **Accounting for Merchandise Purchases**—Perpetual Inventory System

A. The cost of merchandise bought for resale: debit Merchandise Inventory and credit Accounts Payable. (GST and PST have been omitted; discussion of these is deferred until Appendix 6B.)

B. Purchase Returns and Allowances

1. *Purchase returns* are merchandise received by a purchaser but returned to the supplier.

2. A *purchase allowance* is a reduction in the cost of defective merchandise received by a purchaser from a supplier.

3. A *debit memorandum* is a form issued by the purchaser to inform the supplier of a debit made to the supplier's account.

4. Entry: Debit Accounts Payable (or Cash) and Credit Merchandise Inventory.

C. Trade Discounts—Percentage deductions from list price (catalogue price) to arrive at the intended selling price. Trade discounts are not entered into accounts. Transactions are recorded using invoice price.

D. Purchase Discounts—Credit terms are a listing of the amounts and timing of payments between a buyer and seller; may include a cash discount granted to buyers for payment within a specified period of time called the discount period.

1. Example: 2/10, n/30, allows the buyer to deduct 2% of the invoice amount from the payment if it is paid within 120 days of the invoice date; net amount is due in 30 days.

2. Example: n/EOM (end of month): net amount due in 30 days.

3. Entry for payment within discount period: Debit Accounts Payable (full invoice amount), Credit Cash (amount paid = invoice – discount), Credit Merchandise Inventory (amount of discount).

E. Managing Discounts—Most companies set up a system to pay invoices with favourable discounts within the discount period, preferably on the last day of a discount period. Missing out on cash discounts can be very expensive.

F. Transfer of Ownership—the point where ownership of merchandise inventory transfers from the buyer to the seller; determines who pays transportation costs.

1. FOB (*free on board*) shipping point—ownership transfers at shipping point; FOB factory

2. FOB destination—buyer accepts ownership at the seller's place of business.

Responsibility for transportation costs follows title or ownership.

G. Transportation Costs

1. Shipping costs on purchases; called *transportation-in* or *freight-in*: include these as part of the cost of merchandise inventory if paid by company.

2. Shipping goods to customers: called *transportation-out* or *freight-out*: record as delivery expense (a selling expense).

   a. Debit Merchandise Inventory, Credit Cash.

VI. Accounting for Merchandise Sales—Perpetual Inventory System

A. Sales Transactions—two parts:

1. Account for revenue—Debit Accounts Receivable (or cash), Credit Sales (both for the invoice amount).

2. Recognize cost—Debit Cost of Goods Sold, Credit Merchandise Inventory (both for the cost of the inventory sold).

B. Sales Discounts—cash discounts granted to customers for payment within the discount period. Recorded upon collection of cash.

1. Collection after discount period—Debit Cash, Credit Accounts Receivable (full invoice amount).

2. Collection within discount period—Debit Cash (invoice amount less discount), Debit Sales Discount (discount amount), Credit Accounts Payable (full invoice amount).

3. Sales Discount is a contra-revenue account—deducted from Sales.

C. Sales Returns and Allowances

1. *Sales returns*—merchandise customers return to the seller after a sale.

2. *Sales allowances*—reductions in the selling price of merchandise sold to customers (damaged merchandise that a customer is willing to purchase if the selling price is decreased).

3. Entry: Debit Sales Returns and Allowances and Credit Accounts Receivable.
   Additional entry if returned merchandise is salable:
   Debit Merchandise Inventory, Credit Cost of Goods Sold.

4. Sales Returns and Allowances, and Sales Discounts, are contra-revenue accounts—deduct from Sales.

5. Net Sales = Sales – (Sales Discount + Sales Returns and Allowances).

6. *Credit memorandum*: prepared by the seller to "credit" or reduce the customer's accounts receivable.

VII. **Additional Merchandising Issues—Perpetual Inventory System**

    A. Adjusting Entries—Generally same as for a service company.

        1. Additional adjustment needed for any inventory loss referred to as *shrinkage.*

        2. Shrinkage is determined by comparing the recorded quantities of inventory with a physical count.

        3. Entry: Debit Cost of Goods Sold, Credit Merchandise Inventory.

    B. Merchandising Cost Flow

        1. Period One: Beginning inventory + Net cost of purchases – Cost of goods sold = Closing inventory.

        2. Period Two: Closing inventory (Period One) becomes Beginning inventory (Period Two) + Net cost of purchases – Cost of goods sold = Closing inventory.

        3. Cost of goods sold for each period is reported on that period's income statement. Closing inventory is reported on the balance sheet for the period.

VIII. **Income Statement Formats**—Perpetual Inventory System. **No** specific format is required in practice. Two common formats:

    A. Multiple-Step—contains more detail than a listing of revenues minus expenses. Shows gross profit as a step towards determining net income. Two formats:

        1. Classified Multiple-Step—used for internal reporting; shows details of net sales; calculates gross profit; separates operating expenses into selling expenses and general and administrative expenses; calculates income from operations, reports other revenues and expenses, and calculates net income. (Exhibit 6.16)

        2. Condensed Multiple-step—does not show details. (Exhibit 1.17)

    B. Single-Step—includes cost of goods sold as an operating expense and shows only one subtotal for total expenses. (Exhibit 6.18)

    C. Gross Margin Ratio: the relation between sales and cost of goods sold.

        1. Calculated as: $\dfrac{\text{Gross Margin}}{\text{Net Sales}}$

        2. Represents the gross profit in each dollar of sales.

IX.   **Closing Entries**—Perpetual Inventory System

A. Similar for merchandising and service companies.

B. Difference: must close temporary accounts (to Income Summary) related to merchandising activities.

   1. Sales, Sales returns and allowances, Sales discounts, Cost of goods sold

X.   **Periodic and Perpetual Inventory Systems: Accounting Comparisons (Appendix 6A)**

A. Periodic inventory system: merchandise inventory account is updated only once each accounting period, at the end of the period.

B. *Purchases*: debit all merchandise purchases at their cost.

C. *Purchase returns and allowances*: credit cost of defective merchandise.

D. *Purchase discount*: credit discounts taken on purchase transactions.

E. *Transportation*-in: charges to haul merchandise to the store.

F. *End of period*: close Purchases, Purchase returns and allowances, Purchase discounts, and Transportation-in.

G. The inventory account can be updated as part of the adjusting or closing process.

XI.   **Sales Tax (Appendix 6B)**

A. Provincial Sales Tax (PST): a consumption tax applied on sales to the final consumer of products and/or services. PST paid is part of the expense or asset cost associated with purchases.

B. Goods and Services Tax (GST): a 7% consumer tax on almost all goods and services provided in Canada; businesses collect GST on sales, receive full credit for GST paid on purchases, then remit the difference to the appropriate federal authority.

Z-MART
Income Statement
For the Year Ended December 31, 2005

Sales			$321,000
Less: Sales discounts		4,300	
Sales returns and allowances		2,000	6,300
Net sales			$314,700
Cost of goods sold			
Merchandise inventory, December 31,2004		$ 19,000	
Purchases	$235,800		
Less: Purchase returns and allowances	$1,500		
Purchase discounts	4,200	5,700	
Net purchases		$230,100	
Add: Transportation-in		2,300	
Cost of goods purchased		232,400	
Goods available for sale		$251,400	
Merchandise inventory, December 31, 2005		21,000	
Cost of goods sold			230,400
Gross profit from sales			$ 84,300
Operating expenses			
Selling expenses			
Amortization expense, store equipment	$ 3,000		
Sales salaries expense	18,500		
Rent expense, selling space	8,100		
Store supplies expense	1,200		
Advertising expense	11,300		
Total selling expenses		$42,100	
General and administrative expenses			
Amortization expense, office equipment	$ 700		
Office salaries expense	25,300		
Insurance expense	600		
Rent expense, office space	900		
Office supplies expense	1,800		
Total general and administrative expense		29,300	
Total operating expenses			71,400
Income from operations			$12,900
Other revenues and expenses			
Rent revenue		$ 2,800	
Interest expense		(360)	2,440
Net income			$15,340

COMPONENTS OF NET INCOME (FROM OPERATIONS)

		Steps:
(a)	Net Sales	X
(b)	− Cost of Goods Sold*	− X
(c)	Gross Profit on Sales	X
(d)	− Operating Expenses	− X
(e)	Net Income (Loss) from Operations	X

COMPONENTS OF COST OF GOODS SOLD

		Steps:
(a)	Inventory, Beginning of Period	X
(b)	+ Cost of Goods Purchased	+ X
(c)	Cost of Goods Available for Sale	X
(d)	− Inventory, End of Period	− X
(e)	Cost of Goods Sold	X

COMPONENTS OF COST OF GOODS PURCHASED

			Steps:
(a)	Purchases (Periodic Inventory System)		X
(b)	− Purchase Returns & Allowances	X	
	and Purchases Discounts (Periodic)	+ X	− X
(c)	Net Purchases (Periodic)		X
(d)	+ Transportation In		+ X
(e)	Cost of Goods Purchased		X

* Perpetual Inventory Systems have a cost of goods sold account that continuously accumulates costs as items are sold. In a Periodic System this amount is calculated at end of period.

ACCOUNTS USED IN BASIC MERCHANDISING TRANSACTIONS WITH A PERIODIC INVENTORY SYSTEM

ASSETS	LIABILITIES	REVENUES & CONTRA-REV.	COST & CONTRA-COST
Cash Dr. Bal.	Accounts Payable Cr. Bal.	Sales Cr. Bal.	Purchases Dr. Bal.
Accounts Receivable Dr. Bal.		Sales Returns & Allowances Dr. Bal.	Purchase Returns & Allowances Cr. Bal.

EXPENSE

Merchandise Inventory Dr. Bal.	Delivery Expense Dr. Bal.	Sales Discounts Dr. Bal.	Purchase Discounts Cr. Bal.
			Transportation In Dr. Bal.

Note: All Problems assume a perpetual inventory system is used unless identified as an appendix problem. Appendix problem assumes a periodic inventory system.

Problem I

The following statements are either true or false. Place a (T) in the parentheses before each true statement and an (F) before each false statement.

1. ( ) Sales returns and allowances or discounts are not included in the calculation of net sales.
2. ( ) On a classified multiple-step Income Statement, ending merchandise inventory is subtracted from the cost of goods available for sale to determine cost of goods sold.
3. ( ) Net sales minus cost of goods sold is gross profit on sales.
4. ( ) The Balance Sheet for a merchandising business is generally the same as a service business with the exception of the addition of one account.
5. ( ) The gross margin ratio is calculated dividing gross margin by net cost of goods sold.
6. ( ) A perpetual inventory system requires updating the merchandise inventory at the fiscal period end.
7. ( ) Cash discounts on merchandise purchased are debited to the merchandise inventory account.
8. ( ) Transportation costs on merchandise purchased are debited to the merchandise inventory account.
9. ( ) A purchase allowance is an addition to the cost of merchandise by a purchaser.
10. ( ) Recording the purchase of merchandise on account requires a debit to the merchandise inventory account and a credit to accounts payable.

Problem II

You are given several words, phrases, or numbers to choose from in completing each of the following statements or in answering the following questions. In each case select the one that best completes the statement or answers the question and place its letter in the answer space provided.

_____1.   A method of accounting for inventories in which cost of goods sold is recorded each time a sale is made and an up-to-date record of goods on hand is maintained is called a:

    a. product inventory system.
    b. perpetual inventory system.
    c. periodic inventory system.
    d. parallel inventory system.
    e. principal inventory system.

_____2.   Based on the following information, calculate the missing amounts.

Sales	$28,800	Cost of goods sold	?
Beginning inventory	?	Gross profit	$10,800
Purchases	18,000	Expenses	?
Ending inventory	12,600	Net income	3,600

    a.   Beginning inventory, $16,200; Cost of goods sold, $12,600; Expenses, $1,800.
    b.   Beginning inventory, $23,400; Cost of goods sold, $10,800; Expenses, $7,200.
    c.   Beginning inventory, $9,000; Cost of goods sold, $14,400; Expenses, $3,600.
    d.   Beginning inventory, $12,600; Cost of goods sold, $18,000; Expenses, $7,200.
    e.   Beginning inventory, $19,800; Cost of goods sold, $25,200; Expenses, $14,400.

3. What is the effect on the income statement at the end of an accounting period in which the ending inventory of the prior period was overstated and carried forward incorrectly?
   a. Cost of goods sold is overstated and net income is understated.
   b. Cost of goods sold is understated and net income is understated.
   c. Cost of goods sold is understated and net income is overstated.
   d. Cost of goods sold is overstated and net income is overstated.
   e. The errors of the prior period and the current period offset each other, so there is no effect on the income statement.

4. The following information is taken from a proprietorship's income statement. Calculate ending inventory for the business.

Sales	$165,250	Purchase returns	$ 390
Sales returns	980	Purchase discounts	1,630
Sales discounts	1,960	Transportation-in	700
Beginning inventory	16,880	Gross profit	58,210
Purchases	108,380	Net income	17,360

   a. $19,840.
   b. $22,080.
   c. $21,160.
   d. $44,250.
   e. Some other amount.

5. On July 18, Triple Digit Sales Company sold merchandise on credit, terms 2/10, n/30, $1,080. On July 21, Triple Digit issued a $180 credit memorandum to the customer of July 18 who returned a portion of the merchandise purchased. In addition to the journal entry that debits inventory and credits cost of goods sold what other journal entry is necessary to record the July 21 transaction?

   a. Accounts Receivable 180.00
        Sales 180.00
   b. Sales Returns and Allowances.. 180.00
        Accounts Receivable 180.00
   c. Accounts Receivable 900.00
        Sales Returns and Allowances.. 180.00
        Sales 1,080.00
   d. Sales 180.00
        Accounts Receivable 180.00
   e. Sales Returns and Allowances.. 180.00
        Sales 180.00

6. The following information is available from Foster Company

Sales	$110,400
Sales discounts	6,325
Sales returns and allowances	5,650
Merchandise inventory, December 31, 2005	25,000
Merchandise inventory, December 31, 2006	27,000
Purchases	63,000

   Foster's gross margin ratio is:
   a. 38.0%
   b. 44.7%
   c. 50.2%
   d. 57.1%
   e. 64.0%

Problem III

Many of the important ideas and concepts discussed in Chapter 6 are reflected in the following list of key terms. Test your understanding of these terms by matching the appropriate definitions with the terms. Record the number identifying the most appropriate definition in the blank space next to each term.

	Cash discount		List price
	Catalogue price		Merchandise
	Classified, multiple-step income statement		Merchandiser
	Cost of goods sold		Merchandise inventory
	Credit memorandum		Periodic inventory system
	Credit period		Perpetual inventory system
	Credit terms		Provincial Sales Tax (PST)
	Debit memorandum		Purchase discount
	Discount period		Purchase returns and allowances
	EOM		Retailer
	FOB		Sales discount
	Freight-in		Sales returns and allowances
	Freight-out		Selling expenses
	General and administrative expenses		Shrinkage
	Goods and Services Tax (GST)		Single-step income statement
	Gross margin		Trade discount
	Gross margin ratio		Transportation-in
	Gross profit		Transportation-out
	Gross profit ratio		Wholesaler

1. The cost of merchandise sold to customers during a period.

2. A method of accounting that records the cost of inventory purchased but does not track the quantity on hand or sold to customers; the records are updated at the end of each period to reflect the results of physical counts of the items on hand.

3. A term used by a purchaser to describe a cash discount granted to the purchaser for paying within the discount period.

4. The abbreviation for free on board, the designated point at which ownership of goods passes to the buyer; FOB shipping point (or factory) means that the buyer pays the shipping costs and accepts ownership of the goods at the seller's place of business; FOB destination means that the seller pays the shipping costs and the ownership of the goods transfers to the buyer at the buyer's place of business.

5. A middleman that buys products from manufacturers or wholesalers and sells them to consumers.

6. The cost to the purchaser to transport merchandise purchased to the purchaser; transportation-in is part of Cost of Goods Sold.

7. The time period in which a cash discount is available and a reduced payment can be made by the buyer.

8. A middleman that buys products from manufacturers or other wholesalers and sells them to retailers or other wholesalers.

9. Gross profit (net sales minus cost of goods sold) divided by net sales; also called gross margin ratio.

10. A reduction in the price of merchandise that is granted by a seller to a purchaser in exchange for the purchaser paying within a specified period of time called the discount period.

11. A method of accounting that maintains continuous records of the cost of inventory on hand and the cost of goods sold.

12. Another name for transportation-in.

13. A term used by a seller to describe a cash discount granted to customers for paying within the discount period.

14. A federal tax on almost all goods and services provided in Canada.

15. Products, also called goods, that a company acquires for the purpose of reselling them to customers.

16. A notification that the sender has entered a credit in the recipient's account maintained by the sender.

17. Expenses that support the overall operations of a business and include the expenses of such activities as providing accounting services, human resource management, and financial management.

18. A contra revenue account in which sales returns and/or sales allowances are recorded.

19. A contra expense account used when a periodic inventory system is in place in which purchase returns and/or purchase allowances are recorded.

20. A reduction below a list or catalogue price that may vary in amount for wholesalers, retailers, and final consumers.

21. The description of the amounts and timing of payments that a buyer agrees to make in the future.

22. Earns net income by buying and selling merchandise.

23. Another name for list price.

24. A consumption tax applied on sales to the final consumers of products and/or services.

25. Inventory losses that occur as a result of shoplifting or deterioration.

26. The abbreviation for end of month, used to describe credit terms for some transactions.

27. The cost to the seller to transport merchandise sold to the customer; a selling expense.

28. An income statement format that shows intermediate totals between sales and net income and detailed computations of net sales and cost of goods sold.

29. Products that a company owns for the purpose of selling them to customers.

30. Another name for transportation-out.

31. The expenses of promoting sales by displaying and advertising the merchandise, making sales, and delivering goods to customers.

32. An income statement format that includes costs of goods sold as an operating expense and shows only one subtotal for total expenses.

33. The difference between net sales and the cost of goods sold.

34. The time period that can pass before a customer's payment is due.

35. Another name for gross profit ratio.

36. A notification that the sender has entered a debit in the recipient's account maintained by the sender.

37. The difference between net sales and the cost of goods sold.

38. The catalogue price of an item before any trade discount is deducted.

Problem IV

The following amounts appeared on Greens 'N Groceries adjusted trial balance as of December 31, 2006, the end of its fiscal year:

	Debit	Credit
Cash..	$ 4,000	
Merchandise inventory	15,000	
Other assets	8,000	
Liabilities		$ 4,000
Lorne Green, capital		22,300
Lorne Green, withdrawals	10,000	
Sales		80,000
Sales returns and allowances	600	
Cost of goods sold...	47,700	
General and administrative expenses	8,000	
Selling expenses	13,000	
Totals..	$106,300	$106,300

On January 1, 2006, the company's merchandise inventory amounted to $13,000. On December 31, 2006, the company's merchandise inventory amounted to $13,000. *Supplementary records* of merchandising activities during the 2006 year disclosed the following:

Invoice cost of merchandise purchases	$48,500
Purchase discounts received	900
Purchase returns and allowances received	400
Cost of transportation-in	2,500

Required

1. Using the supplementary record information, verify the total amount for the Cost of Goods Sold amount.

2. Using the data above, complete the Income Statement for Greens 'N Groceries for December 31, 2006. Use the form provided on the following page.

COST OF GOODS SOLD:

Merchandise inventory, December 31, 2005								
Purchases								
Less: Purchases returns								
and allowances $_____								
Purchase discounts _____								
Net purchases								
Add: Transportation-in								
Cost of goods purchased								
Goods available for sale								
Merchandise inventory, December 31, 2006								
Cost of goods sold								

GREENS 'N GROCERIES

Income Statement

For the Year Ended December 31, 2006

Revenue:								
Sales								
Less: Sales returns and allowances								
Net sales								
Cost of goods sold								
Gross profit from sales								
Operating expenses:								
Selling expenses								
General and administrative expenses								
Total operating expenses								
Net income								

Problem V

Use the adjusted trial balance presented above to prepare the closing entries for Greens 'N Groceries. Do not give explanations, but skip a line after each entry.

GENERAL JOURNAL   Page 1

DATE	ACCOUNT TITLES AND EXPLANATION	P.R.	DEBIT	CREDIT

Problem VI

1. If a company determines cost of goods sold by counting the inventory at the end of the period and subtracting the inventory from the cost of goods available for sale, the system of accounting for inventories is called a(n)_____.

2. Trade discounts _____ (are, are not) credited to the Inventory account.

3. A reduction in a payable that is granted if it is paid within the discount period is a _____ discount.

4. A store received a credit memorandum from a wholesaler for unsatisfactory merchandise the store sent back for credit. The store should record the memorandum with a _____ (debit, credit) to its Inventory account and a _____ (debit, credit) to its Accounts Payable account.

5. FOB _____ means the buyer accepts ownership at the seller's place of business. FOB _____ means ownership of the goods transfer to the buyer at the buyer's place of business.

Problem VII (Appendix 6A)

The trial balance that follows was taken from the ledger of Wizard Hobbies at the end of its annual accounting period. Jules Wizard, the owner of Wizard Hobbies, did not make additional investments in the business during 2005.

WIZARD HOBBIES
Unadjusted Trial Balance
December 31, 2005

Cash	$1,840	
Accounts receivable	2,530	
Merchandise inventory	3,680	
Store supplies	2,070	
Accounts payable		$4,370
Salaries payable	—	—
Jules Wizard, capital		5,980
Jules Wizard, withdrawals	1,380	
Sales		14,260
Sales returns and allowances	1,150	
Purchases	5,750	
Purchase discounts		920
Transportation-in	1,150	
Salaries expense	4,370	
Rent expense	1,610	
Store supplies expense	—	—
Totals	$25,530	$25,530

Use the adjusting entry approach to account for merchandise inventories and prepare adjusting journal entries and closing journal entries for Wizard Hobbies using the following information:

a. Ending store supplies inventory, $1,150.
b. Accrued salaries payable, $690.
c. Ending merchandise inventory, $4,830.

DATE	ACCOUNT TITLES AND EXPLANATION	P.R.	DEBIT	CREDIT

Solutions for Chapter 6

Problem I

1.	F	6.	F
2.	T	7.	F
3.	T	8.	T
4.	T	9.	F
5.	F	10.	T

Problem II

1. B
2. D
3. A
4. A
5. B
6. A

Problem III

10	Cash discount	38	List price
23	Catalogue price	15	Merchandise
28	Classified, multiple-step income statement	22	Merchandiser
1	Cost of goods sold	29	Merchandise inventory
16	Credit memorandum	2	Periodic inventory system
34	Credit period	11	Perpetual inventory system
21	Credit terms	24	Provincial Sales Tax (PST)
36	Debit memorandum	3	Purchase discount
7	Discount period	19	Purchase returns and allowances
26	EOM	5	Retailer
4	FOB	13	Sales discount
12	Freight-in	18	Sales returns and allowances
30	Freight-out	31	Selling expenses
17	General and administrative expenses	25	Shrinkage
14	Goods and Services Tax (GST)	32	Single-step income statement
33	Gross margin	20	Trade discount
9	Gross margin ratio	6	Transportation-in
37	Gross profit	27	Transportation-out
35	Gross profit ratio	8	Wholesaler

Problem IV

1. COST OF GOODS SOLD:

Merchandise inventory, December 31, 2005											$13	0	0	0	00
Purchases						$48	5	0	0	00					
Less: Purchases returns															
and allowances $_____	$4	0	0	00											
Purchase discounts _____	9	0	0	00		(1	3	0	0	00)					
Net purchases						47	2	0	0	00					
Add: Transportation-in						2	5	0	0	00					
Cost of goods purchased											49	7	0	0	00
Goods available for sale											62	7	0	0	00
Merchandise inventory, December 31, 2006											15	0	0	0	00
Cost of goods sold											$47	7	0	0	00

GREENS 'N GROCERIES
Income Statement
For the Year Ended December 31, 2006

Revenue:..		
Sales	$80,000	
Less: Sales returns and allowances......................................	600	
Net sales...		$79,400
Cost of goods sold...		47,700
Gross profit from sales		31,700
Operating expenses:		
Selling expenses..	$ 8,000	
General and administrative expenses	13,000	
Total operating expenses		21,000
Net income		$10,700

© McGraw-Hill Ryerson, Inc., 2005

Problem V

Date	Account	Debit	Credit
Dec. 31	Sales	80,000.00	
	Income Summary		80,000.00
31	Income Summary	69,300.00	
	Sales Returns and Allowances		600.00
	Cost of Goods Sold		47,700.00
	General and Administrative Expenses		8,000.00
	Selling Expenses		13,000.00
31	Income Summary	10,700.00	
	Lorne Green, Capital		10,700.00
31	Lorne Green, Capital	10,000.00	
	Lorne Green, Withdrawals		10,000.00

Problem VI

1. periodic inventory system

2. are not

3. cash

4. credit, debit

5. shipping point, destination

Problem VII (Appendix 6A)

Adjusting Entries

Dec. 31	Store Supplies Expense		920.00	
	Store Supplies			920.00
31	Salaries Expense		690.00	
	Salaries Payable			690.00
31	Income Summary		3,680.00	
	Merchandise Inventory			3,680.00
31	Merchandise Inventory		4,830.00	
	Income Summary			4,830.00

Closing Entries

Dec. 31	Sales		14,260.00	
	Purchase Discounts		920.00	
	Income Summary			15,180.00
31	Income Summary		15,640.00	
	Sales Returns and Allowances			1,150.00
	Purchases			5,750.00
	Transportation-in			1,150.00
	Salaries Expense			5,060.00
	Rent Expense			1,610.00
	Store Supplies Expense			920.00
31	Income Summary		690.00	
	Jules Wizard, Capital			690.00
31	Jules Wizard, Capital		1,380.00	
	Jules Wizard, Withdrawals			1,380.00

Learning Objective 1:

Identify the costs included in merchandise inventory.

Summary

Merchandise inventory comprises goods owned by a company and held for resale. Goods in transit are reported in inventory of the company that holds ownership rights. Goods out on consignment are reported in inventory of the consignor. Goods damaged or obsolete are reported in inventory at a conservative estimate of their net realizable value, computed as sales price minus the selling costs.

Learning Objective 2:

Identify the costs of merchandise inventory.

Summary

Costs of merchandise inventory comprise expenditures necessary, directly or indirectly, in bringing an item to a saleable condition and location. This means the cost of an inventory item includes its invoice price minus any discount, plus any added or incidental costs necessary to put it in a place and condition for sale.

Learning Objective 3:

Compute cost of goods sold and ending merchandise inventory in a perpetual system using the methods of specific identification, moving weighted average, FIFO, and LIFO.

Summary

Costs are assigned to the cost of goods sold account each time that a sale occurs in a perpetual system. Specific identification assigns costs by referring to the actual cost of the unit sold. Moving weighted average assigns a weighted average cost per unit calculated by taking the current balance in the merchandise inventory account and dividing it by the total items available for sale to determine the weighted average cost per unit. FIFO assigns cost assuming units purchased earliest are the first units sold. LIFO assigns cost assuming the most recently purchased units are the first units sold.

Learning Objective 4:

Analyze the effects of the choice between inventory costing methods on financial reporting.

Summary

When purchase prices are rising or falling, the inventory methods are likely to assign different cost amounts. Specific identification exactly matches costs and revenues. Moving weighted average smoothes out price changes. FIFO assigns an amount to inventory closely approximating current replacement cost. LIFO assigns the most recent costs incurred to cost of goods sold, and likely better matches current costs with revenues. The method(s) used must be disclosed in the notes to the financial statements and be consistent from period to period.

Fundamental Accounting Principles, 11th Canadian Edition

Learning Objective 5:

Compute the lower of cost or market value of inventory.

Summary

Inventory is reported at market value when market is lower than cost. This is called the lower of cost or market (LCM) value of inventory. Market may be measured as net realizable value or replacement cost. Lower of cost or market can be applied separately to each item, to major categories of items, or to the whole of inventory.

Learning Objective 6:

Analyze the effects of inventory errors on current and future financial statements.

Summary

An error in the amount of ending inventory affects assets (inventory), net income (cost of goods sold), and owner's equity of that period. Since ending inventory is next period's beginning inventory, an error in ending inventory affects next period's cost of goods sold and net income. The financial statement effects of errors in one period are offset (reversed) in the next.

Learning Objective 7:

Apply both the gross profit and retail inventory methods to estimate inventory.

Summary

The gross profit method involves two computations: (1) net sales at retail multiplied by the gross profit ratio gives estimated cost of goods sold, and (2) goods available at cost minus estimated cost of goods sold gives estimated ending inventory at cost. The retail inventory method involves three computations: (1) goods available at retail minus net sales at retail gives ending inventory at retail, (2) goods available at cost divided by goods available at retail gives the cost to retail ratio, and (3) ending inventory at retail is multiplied by the cost to retail ratio to give estimated ending inventory at cost.

Learning Objective 8 (Appendix 7A):

Compute inventory in a periodic system using the costing methods of specific identification, weighted average, FIFO, and LIFO.

Summary

Periodic systems allocate the cost of goods available for sale between cost of goods sold and ending inventory *at the end of a period*. Specific identification and FIFO give identical results whether the periodic or perpetual system is used. LIFO assigns cost to cost of goods sold assuming the last units purchased for the period are the first units sold. Weighted average cost computes cost per unit by taking the total cost of both beginning inventory and net purchases and dividing by the total number of units available. It then multiplies cost per unit by the number of units sold to give cost of goods sold.

Learning Objective 9 (Appendix 7B):

Assess inventory management using both merchandise turnover and days' sales in inventory.

Summary

We prefer a high merchandise turnover provided inventory is not out of stock and customers are not being turned away. We use days' sales in inventory to assess the likelihood of inventory being out of stock. We prefer a small number of days' sales in inventory provided we can serve customer needs and provide a buffer for uncertainties. Together, each of these ratios helps us assess inventory management and evaluate a company's short-term liquidity.

Chapter Outline

I. **Inventory Items and Costs**
   A. Merchandise Inventory—includes all goods owned by a company and held for sale.
      1. Goods in transit—included if the rights and risks of ownership have passed (Terms: FOB shipping point).
      2. Goods on consignment—owned by consignor.
      3. Goods damaged or obsolete—included if salable at a conservative estimate of their *net realizable value* (sales price minus the cost of making the sale).

II. **Costs of Merchandise Inventory**
   A. Includes those expenditures necessary, directly or indirectly, in bringing an item to a saleable condition and location.
      1. Cost example: invoice price, minus discount, plus costs necessary to put it in a place and condition for sale, such as import duties, transportation-in, storage, insurance, etc.
      2. Exception: Under the *materiality principle* or the *cost-to-benefit constraint* (effort outweighs benefit), incidental costs of acquiring inventory may be immaterial and are then allocated to cost of goods sold in the period when they are incurred.
   B. Physical Count Merchandise of Inventory
      1. Generally taken at the end of its fiscal year or when inventory amounts are low.
      2. Used to adjust the Merchandise Inventory account balance to the actual inventory on hand; debit Cost of Goods Sold and credit Merchandise Inventory if physical count is less than unadjusted balance of account. Differences occur because of theft, loss, damage and errors.

III. **Assigning Costs to Inventory**—Perpetual Inventory System
   A. Inventory Systems:
      1. Perpetual Inventory—Record cost of goods sold and reductions in inventory as sales occur; shown in chapter.
      2. Periodic Inventory— Determine cost of goods sold and inventory amounts at the end of a period; shown in appendix.
   B. Four methods of assigning costs to inventory and cost of goods sold:
      1. Specific Identification—or, specific invoice inventory pricing, costs directly identified with a specific purchase and its invoice.
      2. Moving Weighted Average—(called weighted average in a periodic inventory costing system) computes the average cost per unit of merchandise inventory at time of each purchase.
      3. First-in, First-out (FIFO)—assumes inventory items are sold in the order acquired; costs of the earliest units purchased are charged to cost of goods sold, leaving costs of most recent purchases in inventory.

    4.   Last-in, First-out (LIFO)—assumes that the most recently purchased units are sold first and charged to cost of goods sold; earliest purchases are assigned to inventory.

  C. Inventory Costing and Technology—advances in information and computing technology have reduced the cost of an electronic perpetual inventory system. Timely access to information is being used strategically by companies to gain a competitive advantage.

IV. Financial Reporting and Inventory

  A. The *full-disclosure principle (GAAP)* requires financial statements to report all relevant information about the operations and financial position of the entity. The inventory costing method used must be disclosed in the notes to the financial statements.

  B. The *consistency principle* (GAAP) requires that a company use the same accounting methods period after period so that the financials statements are comparable across periods; applies to all accounting methods; does not require a company to use one method exclusively.

V. Lower of Cost or Market (LCM)— The *conservatism principle* requires that inventory be reported at market value when market is *lower* than cost. Merchandise inventory is then reported at the lower of cost or market.

    1.   Market: defined as net realizable value (NRV) (selling price less any costs to sell), or current replacement cost.

    2.   The decline from cost to market is recorded in an adjusting entry at the end of the period.

    3.   LCM is applied as one of:

        a.   Separately to each individual item,

        b.   To major categories of items, or

        c.   To the whole inventory

VI.   Errors in Reporting Inventory

    1.   Inventory errors cause misstatements of cost of goods sold, gross profit, net income, current assets, and owner's equity.

    2.   Misstatements will exist in next period's statements because ending inventory of one period is the beginning inventory of the next.

    3.   Because an inventory error causes an offsetting error in the next period, it is said to be self-correcting.

Chapter Outline

Notes

VII. Estimating Inventory

a. Gross profit method—estimates the cost of ending inventory by applying the gross profit ratio (gross margin ratio) to net sales (at retail).

1. Recognize the gross profit portion on each dollar of net sales.
2. Calculate CGS percentage (100% less gross profit percentage)
3. Sales multiplied by CGS percentage = CGS
4. CGA – CGS = estimated ending inventory at cost

B. Retail Inventory Method—estimates the cost of ending inventory for interim statements in a periodic inventory when a physical count is taken only annually. *Steps:*

1. Goods available for sale at retail – Net sales at retail = Ending inventory at retail.
2. Goods available for sale at cost ÷ Goods available for sale at retail = Cost to retail ratio
3. Ending inventory at retail × Cost to retail ratio = Estimated ending inventory at cost

Note: The cost to retail ratio can also be used to convert a physical inventory taken using retail price to cost. Inventory shrinkage can be measured by comparing the converted physical inventory to the estimated inventory.

VIII. Appendix 7A—Assigning Costs to Inventory—Periodic System

    A. Results of periodic vs. perpetual by method:

        1. Specific Identification and FIFO—results same as perpetual.

        2. Weighted-Average—cost per unit: multiply the per unit cost for beginning inventory and each particular purchase by their corresponding number of units; then, add these amounts and divide by the total number of units available for sale.

        3. LIFO—two methods may produce different results.

IX.   Appendix 7B—Using the Information—Merchandise Turnover and Days' Sales in Inventory

    A. Merchandise turnover

        1. Inventory turnover: the number of times a company turns over its inventory during a period

        2. Calculated as: Cost of goods sold

                  Average merchandise inventory*

    *Average is computed by adding beginning and ending inventory amounts and dividing the total by 2.

    B. Days' Sales in Inventory

        1. Estimates how many days it will take to convert inventory on hand into accounts receivable or cash.

        2. Calculated as: Ending inventory × 365

                   Cost of goods sold

Schedule of Cost of Goods Available

	Units		Cost		Total
Jan. 1 Beginning Inventory	60	@	$10	=	$ 600
Mar. 27 Purchase	90	@	11	=	990
Aug. 15 Purchase	100	@	13	=	1,300
Nov. 6 Purchase	50	@	16	=	800
	300				$3,690

Cost of goods available for sale $3,690

Methods of Assigning Cost to Units in Ending Inventory

(1) **Specific Identification** — requires that each item in an inventory be assigned its <u>actual</u> invoice cost.

(2) **Weighted-Average** — a weighted-average cost per unit is determined based on total cost and units of goods available for sale. This cost is assigned to units in the ending inventory.

(3) **First-in, First-out (FIFO)** — assumes the first units acquired (beginning inventory) are the first to be sold and that additional sales flow is in the order purchased. Therefore, the costs of the last items received are assigned to the ending inventory.

(4) **Last-in, First-out (LIFO)** — assumes the last units acquired (most recent purchase) are the first units sold. Therefore, the costs of the first items acquired (starting with beginning inventory) are assigned to the ending inventory.

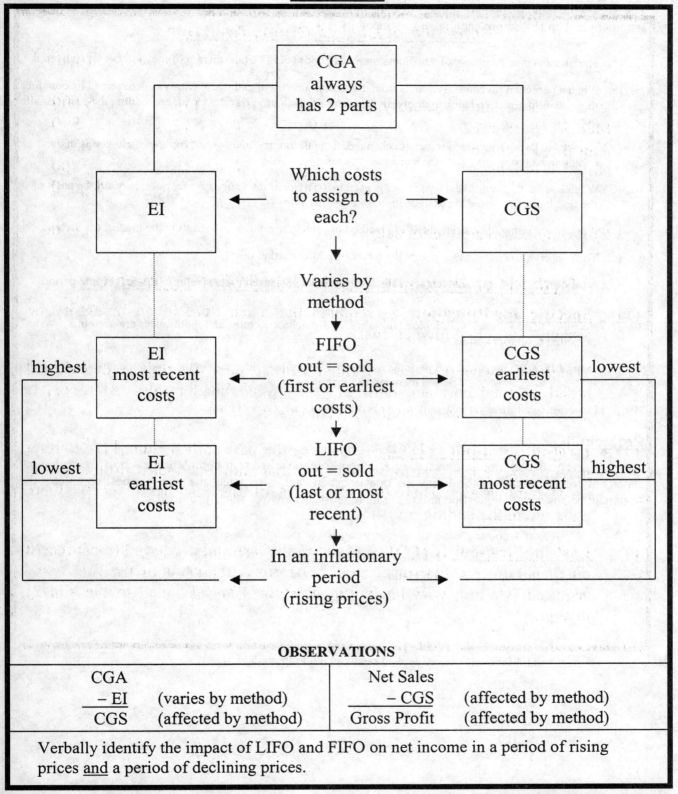

OBSERVATIONS

CGA		Net Sales	
– EI	(varies by method)	– CGS	(affected by method)
CGS	(affected by method)	Gross Profit	(affected by method)

Verbally identify the impact of LIFO and FIFO on net income in a period of rising prices <u>and</u> a period of declining prices.

© *McGraw-Hill Ryerson, Inc.*, 2005

Problem I

The following statements are either true or false. Place a (T) in the parentheses before each true statement and an (F) before each false statement.

1. ( ) The merchandise inventory of a business includes goods sold FOB destination if they are not yet delivered.

2. ( ) When a perpetual inventory system is used, the dollar amount of ending inventory is determined by counting the units of product on hand, multiplying the count for each product by Xs cost, and adding the costs for all products.

3. ( ) If prices of goods purchased remain unchanged, then all four methods of assigning costs to goods in the ending inventory would yield the same cost figures.

4. ( ) When last-in, first-out inventory pricing is used in a perpetual inventory system, as sales occur the costs of the first items purchased are assigned to cost of goods sold.

5. ( ) If prices are rising, then using the FIFO method of pricing inventory will result in the highest net income.

6. ( ) The conservatism principle supports the lower of cost or market rule.

7. ( ) A misstatement of ending inventory will carry forward and cause misstatements in the succeeding period's cost of goods sold, gross profit, and net income.

8. ( ) Accounts titled Purchases, Purchase Discounts, and Purchase Returns and Allowances are used in a perpetual inventory system.

9. ( ) Using LIFO, the perpetual and periodic inventory systems may not result in the same amounts of sales, cost of goods sold, and end-of-period merchandise inventory.

10. ( ) Lower of cost or market may only be applied to major categories of products.

Problem II

You are given several words, phrases, or numbers to choose from in completing each of the following statements or in answering the following questions. In each case select the one that best completes the statement or answers the question and place its letter in the answer space provided.

_____ 1. Retail Company's ending inventory consists of the following:

Product	Units on Hand	Unit Cost	NRV per Unit
X	100	$10	$ 8
Y	90	15	14
Z	75	8	10

Net realizable Value (NRV) is determined to be the best measure of market. Lower of cost or market for the inventory applied separately to each product is:

a. $2,950.

b. $2,810.

c. $2,660.

d. $3,100.

e. $3,160.

The following information is to be used for questions 2 to 5:

Misha Co. made purchases of a particular product in the current year as follows:

Jan.	1	Beginning inventory ...	120 units	@	$5.00	=	$ 600
Mar.	7	Purchased....................	250 units	@	$5.60	=	1,400
July	28	Purchased...................	500 units	@	$5.80	=	2,900
Oct.	3	Purchased...................	450 units	@	$6.00	=	2,700
Dec.	19	Purchased...................	100 units	@	$6.20	=	620
		Total	1,420 units				$8,220

Misha Co. made sales on the following dates at $15 a unit:

Jan.	10	70 units
Mar.	15	125 units
Oct.	5	600 units
Total		795 units

The business uses a perpetual inventory system, and the ending inventory consists of 625 units, 500 from the July 28 purchase and 125 from the Oct. 3 purchase.

_____ 2. Using the specific identification cost assignment method, the amounts to be assigned to cost of goods sold and ending inventory respectively are:

  a. $4,465, $3,755
  b. $4,537.50, $3,682.50
  c. $4,570, $3,650
  d. $4,620, $3,600
  e. $4,570, $3,600

_____ 3. Using the LIFO cost assignment method, the amounts to be assigned to cost of goods sold and ending inventory respectively are:

  a. $4,465, $3,755
  b. $4,537.50, $3,682.50
  c. $4,570, $3,650
  d. $4,620, $3,600
  e. $3,600, $4,620

_____ 4. Using the FIFO cost assignment method, the amounts to be assigned to cost of goods sold and ending inventory respectively are:

  a. $4,465, $3,755
  b. $4,537.50, $3,682.50
  c. $4,570, $3,650
  d. $4,620, $3,600
  e. $4,620, $3,755

_____ 5. Using the weighted-average cost assignment method, the amounts to be assigned to cost of goods sold and ending inventory respectively are:

  a. $4,465, $3,755
  b. $4,537.50, $3,682.50
  c. $4,570, $3,650
  d. $4,620, $3,600
  e. $4,570, $3,682.50

© McGraw-Hill Ryerson, Inc., 2005

7-133

Study Guide, Chapter 7

6. Boston Company uses a perpetual inventory system and made an error at the end of year 1 that caused Atlantis' year 1 ending inventory to be overstated by $5,000. What effect does this error have on the company's financial statements?

    a. Net income is understated; assets are understated.
    b. Net income is understated; assets are overstated.
    c. Net income is overstated; assets are understated.
    d. Net income is overstated; assets are overstated.
    e. Net income is overstated; assets are correctly stated.

7. Due to a fire in the warehouse of David's Company on March 31, all of its inventory was destroyed. The company had an average gross profit rate of 30%. Based on the following information, use the gross profit method to prepare an estimate of the March 31 inventory.

January 1, beginning inventory	$ 85,000
Purchases	197,000
Purchase returns	4,000
Transportation-in	12,000
Sales	385,000
Sales returns	5,000

    a. $ 86,000
    b. $ 90,000
    c. $ 95,000
    d. $102,000
    e. $103,000.

8. Maple Company's ending inventory at December 31, 2006 and 2005, was $210,000 and $146,000, respectively. Cost of goods sold for 2006 was $832,000 and $780,000 for 2005. Calculate Cypress' merchandise turnover for 2006.

    a. 4.7 times
    b. 4.5 times
    c. 4.0 times
    d. 3.8 times
    e. 3.6 times

9. Refer to the information presented in question 8. Calculate Maple's days' sales in inventory for 2006.

    a. 78.1 days.
    b. 80.6 days.
    c. 66.1 days.
    d. 92.1 days.
    e. 68.3 days.

Note: Questions 10–12 relate to Appendix 7A.

_____ 10. Magnum Company began a year and purchased merchandise as follows:

Jan.	1	Beginning inventory	40 units	@	$17.00
Feb.	4	Purchased	80 units	@	$16.00
May	12	Purchased	80 units	@	$16.50
Aug.	9	Purchased	60 units	@	$17.50
Nov.	23	Purchased	100 units	@	$18.00

The company uses a periodic inventory system and the ending inventory consists of 60 units, 20 from each of the last three purchases. Determine ending inventory assuming costs are assigned on the basis of FIFO.

a. $1,040
b. $1,000
c. $1,069
d. $1,080
e. $1,022

_____ 11. Linder Company began a year and purchased merchandise as follows:

Jan.	1	Beginning inventory	40 units	@	$17.00
Feb.	4	Purchased	80 units	@	$16.00
May	12	Purchased	80 units	@	$16.50
Aug.	9	Purchased	60 units	@	$17.50
Nov.	23	Purchased	100 units	@	$18.00

The company uses a periodic inventory system and the ending inventory consists of 60 units, 20 from each of the last three purchases. Determine ending inventory assuming costs are assigned on the basis of LIFO.

a. $1,040.
b. $1,000.
c. $1,022.
d. $980.
e. $1,080.

_____ 12. Crow Company began a year and purchased merchandise as follows:

Jan.	1	Beginning inventory	40 units	@	$17.00
Feb.	4	Purchased	80 units	@	$16.00
May	12	Purchased	80 units	@	$16.50
Aug.	9	Purchased	60 units	@	$17.50
Nov.	23	Purchased	100 units	@	$18.00

The company uses a periodic inventory system and the ending inventory consists of 60 units, 20 from each of the last three purchases. Determine ending inventory assuming costs are assigned on a weighted-average basis.

a. $1,022.00
b. $1,040.00
c. $1,080.00
d. $1,000.00
e. $1,042.50

Problem III

Many of the important ideas and concepts discussed in Chapter 7 are reflected in the following list of key terms. Test your understanding of these terms by matching the appropriate definitions with the terms. Record the number identifying the most appropriate definition in the blank space next to each term.

_____ Conservatism principle	_____ Lower of cost or market (LCM)
_____ Consignee	_____ Market
_____ Consignor	_____ Materiality principle
_____ Consistency principle	_____ Merchandise turnover
_____ Cost-to-benefit constraint	_____ Moving weighted average inventory costing method
_____ Days' sales in inventory	_____ Net realizable value (NRV)
_____ First-in, first-out inventory pricing (FIFO)	_____ Physical count
_____ Full-disclosure principle	_____ Replacement cost
_____ Gross margin ratio	_____ Retail
_____ Gross profit method	_____ Retail inventory method
_____ Gross profit ratio	_____ Specific identification
_____ Internal controls	_____ Specific invoice inventory pricing
_____ Inventory turnover	_____ Taking an inventory
_____ Last-in, first-out inventory pricing (LIFO)	_____ Weighted average
	_____ Weighted average inventory costing method

1. One who receives and holds goods owned by another party for the purpose of selling the goods for the owner.

2. A perpetual inventory pricing system in which the unit cost in inventory is recalculated at the time of each purchase by dividing the total cost of goods available for sale at that point in time by the corresponding total units available for sale. The most current moving weighted average cost per unit is multiplied by the units sold to determine cost of goods sold.

3. The GAAP that requires financial statements (including footnotes) to report all relevant information about the operations and financial position of the entity.

4. The pricing of an inventory where the purchase invoice of each item in the ending inventory is identified and used to determine the cost assigned to the inventory.

5. The pricing of an inventory under the assumption that the items most recently purchased are sold first and their costs are charged to cost of goods sold.

6. The accounting requirement that a company use the same accounting methods period after period so that the financial statements of succeeding periods will be comparable.

7. Either net realizable value or replacement cost.

8. To count merchandise inventory for the purpose of reconciling goods actually on hand to the inventory control account in the general ledger.

9. A periodic inventory pricing system in which the total cost of goods available for sale are divided by the total units available for sale. The resulting weighted average unit cost is multiplied by the units in ending inventory and then to the units that were sold.

10. Measures how much of net sales is gross profit; calculated as gross profit divided by net sales.

11. The selling price of merchandise inventory.

12. The policies and procedures used to protect assets, ensure reliable accounting, promote efficient operations, and urge adherence to company policies.

13. Calculated by dividing the total cost of goods available for sale by the corresponding total units .

14. Current cost of purchasing an item.

15. A procedure for estimating an ending inventory in which the past gross profit rate is used to estimate cost of goods sold, which is then subtracted from the cost of goods available for sale to determine the estimated ending inventory.

16. The pricing of an inventory under the assumption that inventory items are sold in the order acquired; the first items received were the first items sold.

17. This GAAP states that an amount may be ignored if its affect on the financial statements is not important to their users.

18. The accounting principle that guides accountants to select the less optimistic estimate when two estimates of amounts to be received or paid are about equally likely.

19. Another name for the materiality principle.

20. The number of times a company's average inventory was sold during an accounting period, calculated by dividing cost of goods sold by the average merchandise inventory balance.

21. Another name for physical count.

22. The required method of reporting merchandise inventory in the balance sheet where market value is reported when market is lower than cost; the market value may be defined as net realizable value or current replacement cost on the date of the balance sheet.

23. A method for estimating an ending inventory cost based on the ratio of the amount of goods for sale at cost to the amount of goods for sale at marked selling prices.

24. Another name for gross profit ratio.

25. An estimate of how many days it will take to convert the inventory on hand at the end of the period into accounts receivable or cash; calculated by dividing the ending inventory by cost of goods sold and multiplying the result by 365.

26. The expected sales price of an item minus the cost of making the sale.

27. Another name for specific identification.

28. An owner of goods who ships them to another party who will then sell the goods for the owner.

29. Another name for merchandise turnover.

Problem IV

Complete the following by filling in the blanks.

1. Consistency in the use of an inventory costing method is particularly important if there is to be

_____ .

2. If a running record is maintained for each inventory item of the number of units received as units are received, the number of units sold as units are sold, and the number of units remaining after each receipt or sale, the inventory system is called _____ .

3. When a company changes its accounting procedures, the _____
principle requires that the nature of the change, justification for the change, and the effect of the change on _____ be disclosed in the notes accompanying the financial statements.

4. With a periodic inventory system, an error in taking an end-of-period inventory will cause a misstatement of periodic net income for _____ (one, two) accounting periods because _____
_____
_____
_____.

5. When identical items are purchased during an accounting period at different costs, a problem arises as to which costs apply to the ending inventory and which apply to the goods sold. The four commonly used ways of assigning costs to inventory and to goods sold are:

a. _____;

b. _____;

c. _____;

d. _____.

6. A major objective of accounting for inventories is the proper determination of periodic net income through the process of matching _____ and _____. The matching process consists of determining how much of the cost of the goods that were for sale during an accounting period should be deducted from the period's _____ and how much should be carried forward as _____, to be matched against a future period's revenues.

7. Although changing back and forth from one inventory costing method to another might allow management to report the incomes it would prefer, the accounting principle of _____ requires a company to use the same pricing method period after period unless it can justify the change.

8. In the gross profit method of estimating an ending inventory, an average _____ _____ rate is used to determine estimated cost of goods sold, and the ending inventory is then estimated by subtracting estimated _____ from the cost of goods available for sale.

9. In separating cost of goods available for sale into cost of goods sold and cost of goods remaining in inventory, the procedures for assigning a cost to the ending inventory are also the means of determining _____ because whatever portion of the cost of goods available for sale is assigned to ending inventory, the remainder goes to _____.

10. Cost of an inventory item includes _____
_____
_____
_____.

11. Use of the lower-of-cost-or-market rule costs the inventory on the balance sheet using the _____ principle. The argument in favour of this rule provides that any loss should be _____ in the year the loss occurs.

12. When recording a sale of merchandise using a _____ (perpetual, periodic) inventory system, two journal entries must be made. One entry records the revenue received for the sale and the second entry debits the _____ account.

Problem V

A company uses a perpetual inventory system and during a year had the following beginning inventory, purchases, and sales of Product Z:

Jan.	1	Inventory..	200 units	@	$2 =	$400
Mar.	15	Purchased..	400 units	@	$3 =	1,200
Apr.	1	Sold...	300 units			
June	3	Purchased..	200 units	@	$4 =	800
July	1	Sold...	300 units			
Oct.	8	Purchased..	600 units	@	$5 =	3,000
Nov.	1	Sold...	500 units			

In the spaces below show the cost that should be assigned to the ending inventory and to the goods sold under the following assumptions:

	Portions Assigned to—	
	Ending Inventory	Cost of Goods Sold
1. A first-in, first-out (FIFO) basis was used to price the ending inventory	$	$
2. A last-in, first-out (LIFO) basis was used to price the ending inventory	$	$
3. The moving weighted average method was used to price the ending inventory	$	$

Problem VI (Appendix 7B)

Reader's Digest reported the following information for the past year:

Merchandise inventory, beginning of year balance	$28,000
Cost of goods sold	390,000
Merchandise inventory, end of year balance	24,000

Required:

1. Calculate the merchandise inventory turnover.
2. Calculate the days' sales in inventory.

Problem VII

The following end-of-period information about a store's beginning inventory, purchases, and sales is available.

	At Cost	At Retail
Beginning inventory	$ 9,600	$13,000
Net purchases	54,400	69,100
Transportation-in	1,680	
Net sales		69,000

The above information is to be used to estimate the store's ending inventory by the retail method.

1. The store had goods available for sale during the year calculated as follows:

	At Cost	At Retail
Beginning inventory	$_____	$_____
Net purchases	_____	_____
Transportation-in	_____	
Goods available for sale	$_____	$_____

2. The store's cost ratio was: ....

   $_____ / $_____ × 100 = _____

3. Of the goods the store had available for sale at retail prices during the year, the following is gone because of sales at retail .... _____

   Which left the store an estimated ending inventory at retail .... $_____

4. And when the store's cost ratio is applied to this estimated ending inventory at retail, the estimated ending inventory at cost is .... $_____

The store took a physical inventory and counted only $12,850 of merchandise on hand (at retail). Calculate the inventory shortage at cost.

Solutions for Chapter 7

Problem I

1. F	6. T
2. F	7. T
3. T	8. F
4. F	9. T
5. T	10. F

Problem II

1. C	6. D	11. B
2. C	7. B	12. A
3. D	8. A	
4. A	9. D	
5. B	10. D	

Problem III

18	Conservatism principle	22	Lower of cost or market (LCM)
1	Consignee	7	Market
28	Consignor	17	Materiality principle
6	Consistency principle	20	Merchandise turnover
19	Cost-to-benefit constraint	2	Moving weighted average inventory costing method
25	Days' sales in inventory	26	Net realizable value (NRV)
16	First-in, first-out inventory pricing (FIFO)	8	Physical count
3	Full-disclosure principle	14	Replacement cost
15	Gross margin ratio	11	Retail
10	Gross profit method	23	Retail inventory method
24	Gross profit ratio	4	Specific identification
12	Internal controls	27	Specific invoice inventory pricing
29	Inventory turnover	21	Taking an inventory
5	Last-in, first-out inventory pricing (LIFO)	13	Weighted average
		9	Weighted average inventory costing method

Problem IV

1. comparability in the financial statements prepared period after period

2. a perpetual inventory system

3. full-disclosure, net income

4. two, the ending inventory of one period becomes the beginning inventory of the next

5. (a) specific invoice prices; (b) weighted-average cost; (c) first-in, first-out; (d) last-in, first-out

6. costs, revenues, revenues, merchandise inventory

7. consistency

8. gross profit, cost of goods sold

9. cost of goods sold, cost of goods sold

10. the invoice price, less the discount, plus any additional incidental costs necessary to put the item in place and in condition for sale

11. conservatism, recognized

12. perpetual, cost of goods sold

Problem V

	Portions Assigned to—	
	Ending Inventory	Cost of Goods Sold
1.	$1,500	$3,900
2.	900	4,500
3.	1,365	4,035

Problem VI (Appendix 7B)

1. $\dfrac{390,000}{(28,000 + 24,000) / 2}$ = 15 times

2. $\dfrac{24,000}{390,000}$ = 22.46 days, rounded to 23 days.

Problem VII

	At Cost	At Retail
Goods for sale		
Beginning inventory...	$ 9,600	$13,000
Net purchases	54,400	69,100
Transportation-in..	1,680	
Goods available for sale.................................	$65,680	82,100
Cost ratio: $65,680/$82,100 × 100 = 80%.....		
Net sales at retail..		69,000
Ending inventory at retail...............................		$13,100
Ending inventory at cost ($13,100 × 80%)	$10,480	

Inventory shortage at cost:
$13,100 − $12,850 = $250
$250 × 80% = $200

Learning Objective 1:

Explain the relationship of the accounting information system (AIS) to the management information system (MIS).

Summary

The MIS includes the subsystems of Finance, Sales and Marketing, Human Resources, Production, and Accounting. Information systems collect and process data based on inputs for the purpose of generating useful information to both internal and external users.

Learning Objective 2:

Explain the components, structure, and fundamental standards of accounting information systems.

Summary

An AIS collects financial data and processes it through the relevant component: Accounts Payable, Accounts Receivable, Payroll, or a specialty component such as Capital Assets. Computers are invaluable tools in processing data efficiently and effectively. Accounting information systems are guided by five fundamental standards in carrying out their tasks: control, relevance, compatibility, flexibility, and cost-benefit standards.

Learning Objective 3:

Identify what technology-based systems have impacted accounting.

Summary

Source documents are evolving from paper-based to technology-based such as debit card, electronic funds transfer (EFT), and e-commerce transactions. General purpose accounting software is available for small to medium-sized businesses whereas large businesses purchase enterprise-application software programs that can be customized to fit the specific needs of their operation

Learning Objective 4:

Explain the goals and uses of special journals.

Summary

Special journals are used for recording and posting transactions of similar type, with each meant to cover one kind of transaction. Four of the most common special journals are the Sales Journal, Cash Receipts Journal, Purchases Journal, and Cash Disbursements Journal. Special journals are efficient and cost effective tools in helping to journalize and post transactions. In addition, special journals allow an efficient division of labour that is also an effective control procedure.

Learning Objective 5:

Describe the use of controlling accounts and subledgers.

Summary

A General Ledger keeps controlling accounts such as Accounts Receivable or Accounts Payable, but details on individual accounts making up the controlling account are kept in a subledger (such as an Accounts Receivable Subledger). The balance in a controlling account must equal the sum of its subaccount balances after posting is complete.

Learning Objective 6:

Journalize and post transactions using special journals.

Summary

Special journals are devoted to similar kinds of transactions. Transactions are journalized on one line of a special journal, with columns devoted to specific accounts, dates, names, posting references, explanations and other necessary information. Posting is threefold: (1) individual amounts in the Other Accounts column are posted to their General Ledger accounts on a regular (daily) basis, (2) individual amounts in a column that is posted in total to a controlling account at the end of a period (month) are posted regularly (daily) to its account in the subledger, and (3) total amounts for all columns except the Other Accounts column are posted at the end of a period (month) to their column's account title.

Learning Objective 7:

Prepare and test the accuracy of subledgers.

Summary

Account balances in the General Ledger and its subledgers are tested for accuracy after posting is complete. This procedure is twofold: (1) prepare a trial balance of the General Ledger to confirm debits equal credits, and (2) prepare a schedule of a subledger to confirm that the controlling account's balance equals the subledger's balance. A schedule is a listing of accounts from a ledger with their balances and the sum of all balances.

Learning Objective 8 (Appendix 8A):

Apply journalizing and posting of transactions using special journals in a periodic inventory system.

Summary

Transactions are journalized and posted using special journals in a periodic system. The methods are similar to those in a perpetual system. The primary difference is cost of goods sold and inventory do not need adjusting at the time of each sale. This normally results in the deletion of one or more columns in each special journal devoted to these accounts.

Learning Objective 9 (Appendix 8B):

Journalize and post transactions with sales taxes to special journals.

Summary

To facilitate recording of GST and PST in special journals, GST Payable and PST Payable columns must be added to each of the Sales Journal and Cash Receipts Journal, and a GST Receivable column must be added to each of the Purchases Journal and Cash Disbursements Journal.

Chapter Outline

Notes

I.   Information Systems

A. Management Information Systems (MIS) —designed to collect and process data for the purpose of providing users with information. Subsystems are sales and marketing, production, finance, human resources, and accounting.

B. Accounting Information Systems (AIS) —group of components that collect and process raw *financial* data into timely, accurate, relevant, and cost-effective information to meet the purposes of internal and external users. Primary components are accounts payable, accounts receivable, and payroll.

C. Computerizing the AIS has both advantages and disadvantages. (Exhibit 8.3)

D. Structure of an AIS—depends on the requirements of the users.

E. System Standards:

1. Control Standard—requires an AIS to have internal controls, including policies, procedures, and safeguards.

2. Relevance Standard—requires that an AIS report useful, understandable, timely and pertinent information for effective decision making.

3. Compatibility Standard—requires that an AIS conform with a company's activities, personnel, and structure

4. Flexibility Standard—requires that an AIS adapt to changes in the company, business environment, and needs of decision makers.

5. Cost-Benefit Standard—requires that the benefits from each AIS activity outweigh the costs of that activity.

II.   Accounting and Technology

A. Source Documents—provide the basic information processed by accounting system.

B. Computer hardware is the physical equipment in a computerized system.

C. Computer software is the program that directs the operations of computer hardware. Enterprise-application software is an integrated program that manages a company's vital operations from order-taking to manufacturing to accounting.

III. Special Journals in Accounting—Perpetual Inventory Systems

A. General Journal—an all-purpose journal where we can record any transaction.

B. Special Journal—used in recording and posting transactions of similar type. Reduces time and effort in posting.

Chapter Outline

Chapter Outline

Chapter Outline

C. Subsidiary ledger(Subledger)—a listing of individual accounts with common characteristics.

 1. Accounts Receivable Subledger—keeps a separate account for each customer. The single controlling account called Accounts Receivable Control is the summary of the subledger, and is kept in the General Ledger.

 2. Accounts Payable Subledger—keeps a separate account for each creditor. Controlling account is Accounts Payable Control in the General Ledger.

 b. Inventory Subledger—keeps a separate account for each type of inventory. Controlling account is Inventory Control in the General Ledger.

D. Four common special journals:

 1. Sales Journal—records sales of merchandise on credit only. A special Sales Returns and Allowances Journal can be used by a company with large numbers of these items.

 a. End of the period posting—The *total* sales amount is debited to Accounts Receivable and credited to Sales in the General Ledger. The *total* cost amount is debited to Cost of Goods Sold and credited to Inventory.

 b. Individual transactions are typically posted each day to customer accounts in the Accounts Receivable Ledger.

 c. Account balances in the General Ledger and subledgers are tested for accuracy after posting is complete.

 d. Sales returns and allowances—record in the General Journal.

 2. Cash Receipts Journal—records *all* receipts of cash. Must be a columnar journal because different accounts are credited when cash is received from different sources.

 a. Cash from credit customers—payment of a customer's account. Debit Cash and debit Sales Discounts; credit Accounts Receivable.

 b. Cash sales—the amount of the sale is debited to Cash and/or debited to Sales Discounts; and credited to Sales. The cost of sales is debited to Cost of Goods Sold and credited to Inventory.

 c. Only the *totals* of special columns are posted to the General Ledger.

 d. Cash from other sources—use one column for infrequent receipts such as borrowing money, interest on account, or selling unneeded assets. The account numbers for individual posting in the General Ledger are included.

    3. Purchases Journal—used to record all purchases on credit.
- a. Uses a special column to debit Merchandise Inventory for purchases and to credit Accounts Payable. An Other Accounts Debit may be established for other purchases on credit.
- b. The amounts in the Accounts Payable Credit column are posted daily to individual creditor accounts.
- c. Individual amounts in the Other Accounts Debit column usually are posted daily to their General Ledger accounts.
- d. End of period: column totals are posted to their General Ledger Accounts.
- e. Items from the Other Accounts Debit column are posted individually.

    4. Cash Disbursements Journal—used to record all cash payments.
- a. Cheque Register—a cash disbursements journal with a column for cheque numbers.
- b. Amounts in the Other Accounts Debit column posted to their General ledger accounts daily.
- c. Individual amounts posted daily to the specific creditors' accounts in the Accounts Payable Subledger.
- d. End of period: post totals for other columns.

    5. General Journal—used for adjusting, closing, and correcting, and for special transactions not recorded in special journals.

VI. **Appendix 8A—Special Journals under a Periodic System**
- A. Sales Journal—delete the cost of goods sold and merchandise inventory amounts for each sale.
- B. Cash Receipts Journal—delete the cost of goods sold and merchandise inventory amounts for each sale.
- C. Purchases Journal—replace the Merchandise Inventory column with a Purchases column.
- D. Cash Disbursements Journal—replace the Merchandise Inventory column with a Purchase Discounts column.

VII. **Appendix 8B—Special Journals and Sales Taxes**
- A. Sales Tax
  1. Sales Journal and Cash Receipts Journal—separate columns for recording the collection of sales tax (PST) and goods and services tax (GST).
  2. Purchases Journal and Cash Disbursements Journal—separate columns for recording the payment of GST.

Problem I

The following statements are either true or false. Place a (T) in the parentheses before each true statement and an (F) before each false statement.

1. ( ) A Sales Journal is used to record all sales.

2. ( ) At month-end, the total sales recorded in the Sales Journal is debited to Accounts Receivable and credited to Sales.

3. ( ) Sales is a General Ledger account.

4. ( ) Transactions recorded in a journal do not necessarily result in equal debits and credits to General Ledger accounts.

5. ( ) If a general journal entry is used to record a sale on credit, the credit of the entry must be posted twice.

6. ( ) A Management Information System is the vehicle within an organization designed to collect and process data for the purpose of providing information to users.

7. ( ) The primary components within an Accounting Information System are accounts payable, accounts receivable, and payroll.

Problem II

You are given several words, phrases or numbers to choose from in completing each of the following statements or in answering the following questions. In each case select the one that best completes the statement or answers the question and place its letter in the answer space provided.

_____ 1.	A company that uses a Sales Journal, a Purchases Journal, a Cash Receipts Journal, a Cash Disbursements Journal, and a General Journal borrowed $1,500 from the bank in exchange for a note payable to the bank. In which journal would the transaction be recorded?

    a. Sales Journal.
    b. Purchases Journal.
    c. Cash Receipts Journal.
    d. Cash Disbursements Journal.
    e. General Journal.

_____ 2.	A company that uses a Sales Journal, a Purchases Journal, a Cash Receipts Journal, a Cash Disbursements Journal, and a General Journal paid a creditor for office supplies purchased on account. In which journal would the transaction be recorded?

    a. Sales Journal.
    b. Purchases Journal.
    c. Cash Receipts Journal.
    d. Cash Disbursements Journal.
    e. General Journal.

_____ 3.	A book of original entry designed and used for recording only a specified type of transaction is a:

    a. Cheque Register.
    b. Subsidiary Ledger.
    c. General Ledger.
    d. Special Journal.
    e. Schedule of Accounts Payable.

_____ 4. Disadvantages of using a computerized Accounting Information System are:

    a. Greater range and detail of outputs available.

    b. Financial information is immediately available for updating and reporting.

    c. Lower cost of processing each transaction.

    d. Costs related to crashed/crashing systems.

    e. Higher productivity for employees and managers.

Problem III

Many of the important ideas and concepts discussed in Chapter 8 are reflected in the following list of key terms. Test your understanding of these terms by matching the appropriate definitions with the terms. Record the number identifying the most appropriate definition in the blank space next to each term.

_____ Accounting information system (AIS)

_____ Accounts payable subledger

_____ Accounts receivable subledger

_____ Cash disbursements journal

_____ Cash receipts journal

_____ Cheque register

_____ Columnar journal

_____ Compatibility standard

_____ Computer hardware

_____ Computer software

_____ Controlling account

_____ Control standard

_____ Cost-benefit standard

_____ Crossfoot

_____ Enterprise-application software

_____ Flexibility standard

_____ Foot

_____ Management information system (MIS)

_____ Purchases journal

_____ Relevance standard

_____ Sales journal

_____ Schedule of accounts payable

_____ Schedule of accounts receivable

_____ Special journal

_____ Subledger

_____ Subsidiary ledger

1. Any journal that is used for recording and posting transactions of a similar type.

2. A General Ledger account, the balance of which (after posting) equals the sum of the balances of the accounts in a related subsidiary ledger.

3. Another name for a Cash Disbursements journal when the journal has a column for cheque numbers.

4. A subsidiary ledger listing individual credit supplier accounts.

5. A journal used to record sales of merchandise on credit.

6. To add a column of numbers.

7. A listing of individual accounts with a common characteristic.

8. An information system standard requiring that the benefits from an activity in an accounting information system outweigh the costs of that activity.

9. Designed to collect and process data within an organization for the purpose of providing users with information.

10. The people, records, methods, and equipment that collect and process data from transactions and events, organize them in useful forms, and communicate results to decision makers.

11. Programs that manage a company's vital operations, which range from order-taking programs to manufacturing to accounting.

12. A journal that is used to record all purchases on credit.

13. The physical equipment in a computerized accounting information system.

14. A list of the balances of all the accounts in the Accounts Receivable Subledger that is summed to show the total amount of accounts receivable outstanding.

15. An information system standard requiring that an accounting information system aid managers in controlling and monitoring business activities.

16. A subsidiary ledger listing individual credit customer accounts.

17. To add debit and credit column totals and compare the sums for equality.

18. An information system standard requiring that an accounting information system report useful, understandable, timely and pertinent information for effective decision making.

19. A journal with more than one column.

20. Another name for subsidiary ledger.

21. The programs that direct the operations of computer hardware.

22. An information system standard requiring that an information system adapt to changes in the company, business environment, and needs of decisions makers.

23. The special journal that is used to record all receipts of cash.

24. A list of the balances of all the accounts in the Accounts Payable Subledger that is summed to show the total amount of accounts payable outstanding.

25. An information system standard requiring that an accounting information system conform to a company's activities, personnel, and structure.

26. The special journal that is used to record all payments of cash; also called cash payments journal.

© McGraw-Hill Ryerson, Inc., 2005

Problem IV

Complete the following by filling in the blanks.

1. An accounting information system is a group of components that collects and processes _____ into _____ information to meet the purposes of internal and external users.

2. Five fundamental standards of accounting information systems are:

    a. _____

    b. _____

    c. _____

    d. _____

    e. _____

3. When a company records sales returns with general journal entries, the credit of an entry recording such a return is posted to two different accounts. This does not cause the trial balance to be out of balance because_____

    _____.

4. Cash sales _____ (are, are not) normally recorded in the Sales Journal.

5. When special journals are used, credit purchases of store supplies or office supplies should be recorded in the_____.

6. To _____ a column of numbers is to add it. To _____ add the debit column totals and credit column totals and compare the two sums for equality.

7. Cash purchases of store supplies or office supplies should be recorded in a(n)_____

    _____.

8. When a subsidiary Accounts Receivable Ledger is maintained, the equality of the debits and credits posted to the General Ledger is proved by preparing _____. At the same time the balances of the customer accounts in the Accounts Receivable Ledger are proved by preparing_____.

Problem V

Below are nine transactions completed by Dahlia Company on September 30 of this year. Following the transactions are the company's journals with prior September transactions recorded therein.

Requirement One: Record the nine transactions in the company's journals.

Sept. 30   Received an $808.50 cheque from Jack Lee in full payment of the September 20, $825 sale, less the $16.50 discount.
   30   Received a $550 cheque from a tenant in payment of his September rent.
   30   Sold merchandise to Ivy Chong on credit, Invoice No. 655, $1,675.
   30   Received merchandise and an invoice dated September 28, terms 2/10, n/60 from Dhaliwal Company, $4,000.
   30   Purchased store equipment on account from Ohms Company, invoice dated September 30, terms n/10, EOM, $950.
   30   Issued Cheque No. 525 to Madeline Reilly in payment of her $650 salary.
   30   Issued Cheque No. 526 for $1,715 to Ohms Company in full payment of its September 20 invoice, less a $35 discount.
   30   Received a credit memorandum from Ohms Company for unsatisfactory merchandise received on September 24 and returned for credit, $625.
   30   Cash sales for the last half of the month totalled $9,450.50.

DATE	ACCOUNT TITLES AND EXPLANATION	P.R.	DEBIT	CREDIT

SALES JOURNAL   Page 8

DATE		ACCOUNT DEBITED	INVOICE NUMBER	P.R.	Accts Receivable Dr. Sales Cr.				
2005 Sept. 3		L. Sierra	651	√	1	8	7	5	00
	15	Ivy Chong	652	√	1	5	0	0	00
	20	Jack Lee	653	√		8	2	5	00
	24	L. Sierra	654	√	2	2	5	0	00

PURCHASES JOURNAL   Page 8

DATE		ACCOUNT	DATE OF INVOICE	TERMS	P.R.	ACCOUNTS PAYABLE CREDIT					PURCHASES DEBIT					OTHER ACCOUNTS DEBIT			
2005 Sept. 8		Dhaliwal Company	Sept. 6	2/10, n/60	√	3	7	5	0	00	3	7	5	0	00				
	22	Ohms Company	Sept. 20	2/10, n/60	√	1	7	5	0	00	1	7	5	0	00				
	24	Ohms Company	Sept. 22	2/10. n/60	√	5	6	2	5	00	5	6	2	5	00				

CASH RECEIPTS JOURNAL

DATE	ACCOUNT CREDITED	EXPLANATION	P.R.	CASH DEBIT	SALES DISCOUNTS DEBIT	ACCOUNTS RECEIVABLE CREDIT	SALES CREDIT	OTHER ACCOUNT CREDIT
20--								
Sept. 1	Rent Earned	Tenant's September rent	406	5 5 0 00				5 5 0 00
13	L. Sierra	Full payment of account	√	1 8 3 7 50	3 7 50	1 8 7 5 00		
15	Sales	Cash sales	√	9 0 0 0 00			9 0 0 0 00	

Fundamental Accounting Principles, 11th Canadian Edition

ACCOUNTS RECEIVABLE LEDGER

L. Sierra
2200 Elm Street

DATE	EXPLANATION	P.R.	DEBIT					CREDIT					BALANCE				
2005 Sept. 3		S-8	1	8	7	5	00						1	8	7	5	00
13		R-9						1	8	7	5	00					
24		S-8	2	2	5	0	00						2	2	5	0	00

Jack Lee
10765 Maple Avenue

DATE	EXPLANATION	P.R.	DEBIT				CREDIT				BALANCE			
2005 Sept. 20		S-8	8	2	5	00					8	2	5	00

Ivy Chong
785 Dogwood Circle

DATE	EXPLANATION	P.R.	DEBIT					CREDIT					BALANCE				
2005 Sept. 15		S-8	1	5	0	0	00						1	5	0	0	00

ACCOUNTS PAYABLE LEDGER

Dhaliwal Company
118 E. Seventh Street

DATE	EXPLANATION	P.R.	DEBIT					CREDIT					BALANCE				
2005 Sept. 8		P-8						3	7	5	0	00	3	7	5	0	00
16		D-7	3	7	5	0	00							-	0	-	

Ohms Company

788 Hazelwood Avenue

DATE	EXPLANATION	P.R.	DEBIT	CREDIT	BALANCE
2005 Sept. 22		P-8		1 7 5 0 00	1 7 5 0 00
24		p-8		5 6 2 5 00	7 3 7 5 00

GENERAL LEDGER

Cash   Account No. 101

DATE	EXPLANATION	P.R.	DEBIT	CREDIT	BALANCE

Accounts Receivable   Account No. 106

DATE	EXPLANATION	P.R.	DEBIT	CREDIT	BALANCE

Store Equipment   Account No. 165

DATE	EXPLANATION	P.R.	DEBIT	CREDIT	BALANCE

Accounts Payable   Account No. 201

DATE	EXPLANATION	P.R.	DEBIT	CREDIT	BALANCE

Rent Earned   Account No. 406

DATE	EXPLANATION	P.R.	DEBIT	CREDIT	BALANCE
2005 Sept. 1		R-9		5 5 0 00	5 5 0 00

Sales   Account No. 413

DATE	EXPLANATION	P.R.	DEBIT	CREDIT	BALANCE

Sales Discounts   Account No. 415

DATE	EXPLANATION	P.R.	DEBIT	CREDIT	BALANCE

Purchases   Account No. 505

DATE	EXPLANATION	P.R.	DEBIT	CREDIT	BALANCE

Purchases Discounts   Account No. 507

DATE	EXPLANATION	P.R.	DEBIT	CREDIT	BALANCE

Salaries Expense   Account No. 622

DATE	EXPLANATION	P.R.	DEBIT	CREDIT	BALANCE
2005 Sept. 15		D-7	6 5 0 00		6 5 0 00

DAHLIA COMPANY
Trial Balance
September 30, 2005

Account	Debit	Credit
Cash		
Accounts receivable		
Store equipment		
Accounts payable		
Rent earned		
Sales		
Sales discounts		
Purchases		
Purchases discounts		
Salaries expense		

DAHLIA COMPANY

Schedule of Accounts Receivable

September 30, 2005

DAHLIA COMPANY

Schedule of Accounts Payable

September 30, 2005

Solutions for Chapter 8

Problem I

1. F
2. T
3. T
4. F
5. F
6. T
7. T

Problem II

1. C
2. D
3. D
4. D

Problem III

10	Accounting information system (AIS)	17	Crossfoot
4	Accounts payable subledger	11	Enterprise-application software
16	Accounts receivable subledger	22	Flexibility standard
26	Cash disbursements journal	6	Foot
23	Cash receipts journal	9	Management information system (MIS)
3	Cheque register	12	Purchases journal
19	Columnar journal	18	Relevance standard
25	Compatibility standard	5	Sales journal
13	Computer hardware	24	Schedule of accounts payable
21	Computer software	14	Schedule of accounts receivable
2	Controlling account	1	Special journal
15	Control standard	20	Subledger
8	Cost-benefit standard	7	Subsidiary ledger

Problem IV

1. Raw financial data, timely accurate relevant and cost-effective.

2. Control Standard, Relevance Standard, Compatibility Standard, Flexibility Standard, Cost-benefit Standard

3. Only the balance of one of the accounts, the Accounts Receivable account, appears on the trial balance.

4. are not

5. purchases journal

6. foot, crossfoot

7. Cash Disbursements Journal

8. a trial balance, a schedule of accounts receivable

Problem V

Sept 30   Accounts Payable—Ohms Company .... 201/√   625.00

             Purchases Returns and Allowances 506   625.00

SALES JOURNAL   Page 8

DATE	ACCOUNT DEBITED	INVOICE NUMBER	P.R.	Accts Receivable Dr. Sales Cr.				
2005 Sept. 3	L. Sierra	651	√	1	8	7	5	00
15	Ivy Chong	652	√	1	5	0	0	00
20	Jack Lee	653	√		8	2	5	00
24	L. Sierra	654	√	2	2	5	0	00
30	Ivy Chong	655	√	1	6	7	5	00
30	Totals.			8	1	2	5	00
				(106/413)				

PURCHASES JOURNAL   Page 8

DATE	ACCOUNT	DATE OF INVOICE	TERMS	P.R.	ACCOUNTS PAYABLE CREDIT				PURCHASES DEBIT					OTHER ACCOUNTS DEBIT				
2005 Sept. 8	Dhaliwal Company	Sept. 6	2/10, n/60	√	3	7	5	0	00	3	7	5	0	00					
22	Ohms Company	Sept. 20	2/10, n/60	√	1	7	5	0	00	1	7	5	0	00					
24	Ohms Company	Sept. 22	2/10. n/60	√	5	6	2	5	00	5	6	2	5	00					
30	Dhaliwal Company	Sept. 28	2/10, n/60	√	4	0	0	0	00	4	0	0	0	00					
30	Str Equip/Ohms Co.	Sept. 30	n/10, EOM	165√		9	5	0	00						9	5	0	00	
30	Totals				16	0	7	5	00	15	1	2	5	00	9	5	0	00	
					(201)					(505)					(√)				

Fundamental Accounting Principles, 11th Canadian Edition

CASH RECEIPTS JOURNAL

DATE	ACCOUNT CREDITED	P.R.	CASH DEBIT	SALES DISCOUNT DEBIT	ACCOUNTS RECEIVABLE CREDIT	SALES CREDIT	OTHER ACCOUNTS CREDIT
20--							
Sept. 1	Rent Earned	406	5500 00				5500 00
13	L. Sierra	√	1837 50	37 50	1875 00		
15	Sales	√	9000 00			9000 00	
30	Jack Lee	√	808 50	16 50	825 00		
30	Rent Earned	406	5500 00				5500 00
30	Sales	√	9450 50			9450 50	
30	Totals		22196 50	54 00	2700 00	18450 50	11000 00
			(101)	(415)	(106)	(413)	(√)

CASH DISBURSEMENTS JOURNAL

DATE	CH. NO.	PAYEE	ACCOUNT DEBITED	P.R.	CASH CREDIT	PURCHASES DISCOUNTS CREDIT	OTHER ACCOUNTS DEBIT	ACCOUNTS PAYABLE DEBIT
20--								
Sept. 15	523	Madeline Reilly	Salaries Expense	622	650 00		650 00	
16	524	Dhaliwal Company		√	3675 00	75 00		3750 00
30	525	Madeline Reilly	Salaries Expense	622	650 00		650 00	
30	526	Ohms Company		√	1715 00	35 00		1750 00
30		Totals			6690 00	110 00	1300 00	5500 00
					(101)	(507)	(√)	(201)

GENERAL LEDGER

Cash   No. 101

Date	Debit	Credit	Balance
Sept. 30	22,20016.50		22,20016.50
30		6,690.00	15,506.50

Sales   No. 413

Date	Debit	Credit	Balance
Sept. 30		8,125.00	8,125.00
30		18,450.50	26,575.50

Accounts Receivable   No. 106

Date	Debit	Credit	Balance
Sept. 30	8,125.00		8,125.00
30		2,700.00	5,425.00

Sales Discounts   No. 415

Date	Debit	Credit	Balance
Sept. 30	54.00		54.00

Store Equipment   No. 165

Date	Debit	Credit	Balance
Sept. 30	950.00		950.00

Purchases   No. 505

Date	Debit	Credit	Balance
Sept. 30	15,125.00		15,125.00

Accounts Payable   No. 201

Date	Debit	Credit	Balance
Sept. 30		16,075.00	16,075.00
30	5,500.00		10,575.00
30	625.00		9,950.00

Purchases Returns & Allowances   No. 506

Date	Debit	Credit	Balance
Sept. 30		625.00	625.00

Rent Earned   No. 406

Date	Debit	Credit	Balance
Sept. 1		550.00	550.00
30		550.00	1,100.00

Purchases Discounts   No. 507

Date	Debit	Credit	Balance
Sept. 30		110.00	110.00

Salaries Expense   No. 622

Date	Debit	Credit	Balance
Sept. 15	650.00		650.00
30	650.00		1,300.00

ACCOUNTS PAYABLE LEDGER

Dhaliwal Company

Date	Debit	Credit	Balance
Sept. 8		3,750.00	3,750.00
16	3,750.00		-0-
30		4,000.00	4,000.00

Ohms Company

Date	Debit	Credit	Balance
Sept. 22		1,750.00	1,750.00
24		5,625.00	7,375.00
30		950.00	8,325.00
30	1,750.00		6,575.00
30	625.00		5,950.00

ACCOUNTS RECEIVABLE LEDGER

L. Sierra

Date	Debit	Credit	Balance
Sept. 3	1,875.00		1,875.00
13		1,875.00	-0-
24	2,250.00		2,250.00

Ivy Chong

Date	Debit	Credit	Balance
Sept. 15	1,500.00		1,500.00
30	1,675.00	5,625.00	3,175.00

Jack Lee

Date	Debit	Credit	Balance
Sept. 20	825.00		825.00
30		825.00	-0-

DAHLIA COMPANY
Trial Balance
September 30, 2005

Cash	$15,506.50	
Accounts receivable	5,425.00	
Store equipment	950.00	
Accounts payable		$ 9,950.00
Rent earned		1,100.00
Sales		26,575.50
Sales discounts	54.00	
Purchases	15,125.00	
Purchases returns and allowances		625.00
Purchase discounts		110.00
Salaries expense	1,300.00	
Totals	$38,360.50	$38,360.50

DAHLIA COMPANY
Schedule of Accounts Receivable
September 30, 2005

L. Sierra	$2,250.00
Ivy Chong	3,175.00
Total accounts receivable	$5,425.00

DAHLIA COMPANY
Schedule of Accounts Payable
September 30, 2005

Dhaliwal Company	$4,000.00
Ohms Company	5,950.00
Total accounts payable	$9,950.00

CHAPTER 9
INTERNAL CONTROL AND CASH

Learning Objective 1:

Define, explain the purpose, and identify the principles of internal control.

Summary

An internal control system consists of the policies and procedures that managers use to protect assets, ensure reliable accounting, promote efficient operations, and encourage adherence to company policies. It is a key part of systems design, analysis and performance. It can prevent avoidable losses and help managers both plan operations and monitor company and human performance. Principles of good internal control include establishing responsibilities, maintaining adequate records, insuring assets and bonding employees, separating recordkeeping from custody of assets, dividing responsibilities for related transactions, applying technological controls, and performing regular independent reviews.

Learning Objective 2:

Define cash and explain how it is reported.

Summary

Cash includes currency and coins, and amounts on deposit in bank, chequing and some savings accounts. It also includes items that are acceptable for deposit in these accounts. Cash equivalents or short-term investments are similar to cash, therefore most companies combine them with cash as a single item on the balance sheet. Cash and cash equivalents are liquid assets because they are converted easily into other assets or used in paying for services or liabilities.

Learning Objective 3:

Apply internal control to cash.

Summary

Internal control of cash receipts ensures all cash received is properly recorded and deposited. Cash receipts arise from cash sales, collections of customers' accounts, receipts of interest and rent, bank loans, sale of assets, and owner investments. Good internal control for cash receipts by mail includes at least two people being assigned to open the mail and prepare a list with each sender's name, amount of money received, and explanation.

Learning Objective 4:

Explain and record petty cash fund transactions.

Summary

To avoid writing cheques for small amounts, a company sets up one or more petty cash funds to pay for items such as postage, courier fees, repairs and supplies. A petty cash fund cashier is responsible for safekeeping of the cash, for making payments from this fund, and for keeping receipts and records. A Petty Cash account is debited when the fund is established or increased in size. The cashier presents all paid receipts to the company's cashier for reimbursement to restore petty cash to its full amount. Petty cash disbursements are recorded whenever the fund is replenished with debits to expense accounts reflecting receipts and a credit to cash.

Learning Objective 5:

Explain and identify banking activities and the control features they provide.

Summary

Banks offer several basic services such as the bank account, the bank deposit, and chequing, that promote either or both the control or safeguarding of cash. A bank account is set up by a bank and permits a customer to deposit money for safeguarding and cheque withdrawals. A bank deposit is money contributed to the account with a deposit slip as proof. A cheque is a document signed by the depositor instructing the bank to pay a specified amount of money to a designated recipient. Sales resulting from debit card and credit card transactions are deposited into the bank account immediately, less a fee. Electronic funds transfer (EFT) uses electronic communication to transfer cash from one party to another, and it decreases certain risks while exposing others. Companies increasingly use it because of its convenience and low cost.

Learning Objective 6:

Prepare a bank reconciliation and journalize any resulting adjustment(s).

Summary

A bank reconciliation is prepared to prove the accuracy of the depositor's and the bank's records. In completing a reconciliation, the bank statement balance is adjusted for such items as outstanding cheques and unrecorded deposits made on or before the bank statement date but not reflected on the statement. The depositor's cash account balance also often requires adjustment. These adjustments include items such as service charges, bank collections for the depositor, and interest earned on the account balance.

Learning Objective 7 (Appendix 9A):

Compute the acid-test ratio and explain its use as an indicator of a company's liquidity.

Summary

The acid-test ratio is computed as quick assets (cash, short-term investments, and receivables) divided by current liabilities. It is an indicator of a company's ability to pay its current liabilities with its existing quick assets. A ratio equal to or greater than one is often considered adequate.

Chapter Outline

I. **Internal Control**

   A. Purpose—An *internal control system* is all policies and procedures used to:

     1. Protect assets.

     2. Ensure reliable accounting.

     3. Promote efficient operations.

     4. Encourage adherence to company policies.

   B. Principles of Internal Control:

     1. *Ensure transactions and activities are authorized* by establishing responsibilities for each task clearly and for one person.

     2. *Maintain* adequate *records* to help protect assets by ensuring that employees use prescribed procedures.

     3. *Insure assets* and *bond* key employees to reduce risk of loss from casualty and theft.

     4. *Separate recordkeeping and custody of assets* so a person who controls or has access to an asset is not responsible for the maintenance of that asset's accounting records.

     5. Establish a *separation of duties* by dividing responsibility for related transactions between two or more individuals or departments.

     6. *Apply technological controls.*

     7. *Perform regular and independent reviews* to ensure that internal control procedures are followed.

   C. Technology and Internal Control—fundamental principles of internal control are relevant no matter what the technological state of the accounting system. Technological impacts:

     1. Reduced processing errors.

     2. More extensive testing of records.

     3. Limited evidence of processing.

     4. Crucial separation of duties.

   D. Limitations of Internal Control

     1. Human error.

     2. Human fraud.

II.   Cash—Defined

    A. Cash—includes currency, coins, amounts on deposit in bank accounts, chequing accounts and some savings accounts. Also includes items that are acceptable for deposit in these accounts.

    B. *Cash equivalents* are short-term investments, similar to cash and often combined with cash.

    C. *Liquidity* refers to how easily an asset can be converted into another asset or be used in paying for services or obligations. Cash and similar assets are called *liquid assets*.

III.   Control of Cash

    A. Internal cash control procedures should meet three guidelines:

       1. Separate handling of cash from recordkeeping of cash.

       2. Cash receipts are promptly (daily) deposited in a bank.

       3. Cash disbursements are made by cheque.

    B. Control of Cash Receipts—include procedures for protecting:

       1. Over-the-counter cash receipts

         a. Apply internal control principles, and

         b. Record cash shortages and overages.

       2. Cash receipts by mail.

    C. Control of Cash Disbursements—to safeguard against theft:

       1. Requires that all expenditures be made by cheque, with two signatures if possible when not signed by the owner, that person not having access to the accounting records.

       2. Exception—small payments made from *petty cash fund*. Operating a petty cash fund involves:

         a. Establish the fund: debit Petty Cash and credit Cash.

         b. Petty Cashier is responsible for safekeeping of the cash, for making payments from this fund, and keeping accurate records.

         c. Reimbursement—debit the expenses or other items paid for with petty cash and credit Cash for the amount reimbursed to the petty cash fund.

         d. Record petty cash shortages/overages.

         e. Increase or Decrease Fund: debit Petty Cash for the amount of the increase or credit Petty Cash for decrease.

IV.   **Banking Activities as Controls**
   A. Basic Bank Services
       1. Bank Account—permits the customer to deposit money for safeguarding and cheque withdrawals.
       2. Bank Deposit—each bank deposit is supported by a *deposit slip*
       3. Bank Cheque—a document signed by the depositor instructing the bank to pay a specified amount of money to a designated recipient.
       4. Electronic Funds Transfer (EFT)—use of electronic communication to transfer cash from one party to another.
       5. Credit Card Transactions—customer convenience to pay for purchases instead of using cash or cheques. The seller pays a few for the service.
       6. Bank Credit Card (Visa or Mastercard)—the retailer receives cash, net of the credit card fee, immediately upon deposit of the credit card sales receipt at the bank.
       7. Debit Card Transactions—Payment for a purchase is electronically transferred from the customer's bank account to the vendor's bank account immediately at the point of sale.
   B. Bank Statement—shows the activity in the accounts during a month.
   C. *Bank reconciliation*—explains the difference between the balance of a chequing account according to the depositor's records and the balance reported on the bank statement.
       1. Purpose—proves the accuracy of both the deposit's records and those of the bank. The two balances must reconcile.
       2. Factors causing the bank statement balance to differ from the depositor's book balance are:
           a. Unrecorded deposits.
           b. Outstanding cheques.
           c. Additions for collections and for interest.
           d. Deductions for uncollectible items and services.
           e. Errors—by both banks and depositors.

3. Bank Reconciliation—steps in reconciling:

   a. Compare deposits on the bank statement with deposits in the accounting records. Identify discrepancies.

   b. Compare cancelled cheques on the bank statements with actual cheques returned with the statement. List discrepancies or errors.

   c. Compare cancelled cheques on the bank statements with cheques recorded in the books.

   d. Identify outstanding cheques listed on the previous month's bank reconciliation that are not included in this month's cancelled cheques.

   e. Inspect all additions (credits) on the bank statement and determine whether recorded in the books. Include bank collections, correction of errors, interest earned.

   f. Inspect all deductions (debits) on the bank statement and determine whether recorded in the books. Include bank charges, NSF cheques, service charges.

D. Recording adjusting entries from bank reconciliation

1. Additions to book balance are debited to cash. The account credited depends on the reason for the addition. Examples are notes collected by the bank and interest earned.

2. Subtractions from book balance are credited to cash. The account debited depends on the reason for the subtraction. Examples are accounts receivable, for NSF cheques, and service charges.

V. **Using the Information — Acid-Test Ratio (Appendix 9A)**

A. Merchandise inventories, a large part of current assets, are not readily available for paying current liabilities. A measure other than the current ratio is used to obtain a more strict measure of a company's ability to cover current liabilities.

B. Acid-test ratio = $\dfrac{\text{Quick assets*}}{\text{Current liabilities}}$

* Quick assets are cash, short-term investments, and receivables

BANK RECONCILIATION

Reasons for discrepancies between
bank statement balance and chequebook
balance:

Handle as follows:

Unrecorded deposits	Add to bank balance
Outstanding cheques	Deduct from bank balance
Bank service charges	Deduct from book balance
Debit memos	Deduct from book balance
Credit memos	Add to book balance
NSF cheques	Deduct from book balance
Interest	Add to book balance
Electronic funds transfer (EFT)	Add to or deduct from book balance
Errors	Must analyze individually (bank errors affect bank balance and book errors affect book balance)

Problem I

The following statements are either true or false. Place a (T) in the parentheses before each true statement and an (F) before each false statement.

1. ( ) One of the fundamental principles of internal control states that the person who has access to or is responsible for an asset should not maintain the accounting record for that asset.

2. ( ) Procedures for controlling cash disbursements are less important than procedures for controlling cash receipts.

3. ( ) Cash includes currency, coins, and amounts on deposit in bank accounts.

4. ( ) After the petty c ash fund is established, the Petty Cash account is not debited or credited again unless the size of the fund is changed.

5. ( ) The Cash Over and Short account is usually shown on the income statement as part of miscellaneous revenues if it has a credit balance at the end of the period.

6. ( ) If 20 cancelled cheques are listed on the current month's bank statement, then no less than 20 cheques could have been issued during the current month.

7. ( ) If an error is made on the bank statement, then a journal entry is needed.

8. ( ) A cancelled cheque is a cheque that has been cancelled by the bank.

Problem II

You are given several words, phrases, or numbers to choose from in completing each of the following statements or in answering the following questions. In each case select the one that best completes the statement or answers the question and place its letter in the answer space provided.

_____1. One of the following is NOT a fundamental internal control principle:

    a. .Maintain adequate records.

    b. .Separate recordkeeping from custody of assets.

    c. Ensure adequate cash is available to pay liabilities.

    d. .Insure assets and bond key employees.

    e. Establish responsibilities for each task.

_____2. Liquidity is:

    a. The portion of a corporation's equity that represents investments in the corporation by its shareholders.

    b. Cash or other assets that are reasonably expected to be realized in cash or be sold or consumed within one year or one operating cycle of the business.

    c. A characteristic of an asset indicating how easily the asset can be converted into cash or used to buy services or satisfy obligations.

    d. Obligations that are due to be paid or liquidated within one year or one operating cycle of the business.

    e. Economic benefits or resources without physical substance, the value of which stems from the privileges or rights that accrue to their owner.

_____ 3. The purpose of a bank reconciliation is to:

    a. Ensure that all transaction have been properly recorded.

    b. Ensure that only authorized payments have been made.

    c. Prove the accuracy of the depositor's cash records.

    d. Ensure the accuracy of the bank statement.

    e. Ensure that all payments have been made by cheque.

_____ 4. Each of the following items would cause General Goods Company's book balance of cash to differ from its bank statement balance.

    A. A service charge made by the bank.

    B. A cheque listed as outstanding on the previous month's reconciliation and that is still outstanding.

    C. A customer's cheque returned by the bank marked "NSF."

    D. A deposit which was mailed to the bank on the last day of November and is unrecorded on the November bank statement.

    E. A cheque paid by the bank at its correct $422 amount but recorded in error in the General Journal at $442.

    F. An unrecorded purchase paid by debit card.

    G. A cheque written during November and not yet paid and returned by the bank.

    Which of the above items require entries on the books of Brand X Sales Company?

    a. A, B, C, and E

    b. A, C, E, and F

    c. A, B, D, and F

    d. A, B, D, E, and G

    e. C, D, E. and F

    5. A company reported the following year-end account balances for 2006.

Cash	$37,000
Accounts receivable	$33,000
Merchandise Inventory	$45,000
Current liabilities	$78,000

    The acid-test ratio is calculated as:

    a. 0.47

    b. 0.68

    c. 0.90

    d. 1.11

    e. 1.47

Problem III

Many of the important ideas and concepts discussed in Chapter 9 are reflected in the following list of key terms. Test your understanding of these terms by matching the appropriate definitions with the terms. Record the number identifying the most appropriate definition in the blank space next to each term.

_____ Acid-test ratio	_____ Internal control system
_____ Bank reconciliation	_____ Liquid asset
_____ Bond	_____ Liquidity
_____ Cancelled cheques	_____ Petty cashier
_____ Cash	_____ Principles of internal control
_____ Cash Over and Short account	_____ Quick ratio
_____ Cheque	_____ Quick assets
_____ Collusion	_____ Separation of duties
_____ Debit card	_____ Signature card
_____ Deposit slip	_____ Voucher system
_____ Electronic funds transfer	_____

1. An analysis that explains the difference between the balance of chequing account shown in the depositor's records and the balance reported on the bank statement.

2. An asset such as cash that is easily converted into other types of assets or used to buy services or to pay liabilities.

3. Employee responsible for safekeeping of the cash, making payments from this fund, and keeping accurate records.

4. A document signed by the depositor instructing the bank to pay a specified amount of money to a designated recipient.

5. The use electronic communication to transfer cash from one party to another.

6. A set of procedures and approvals designed to control cash disbursements and acceptance of obligations.

7. Card used at point of sale to transfer payment for a purchase immediately from the customer's to the vendor's bank account.

8. All the policies and procedures managers use to protect assets, ensure reliable accounting, promote efficient operations, and urge adherence to company policies.

9. A ratio used to assess a company's ability to cover its current debts with existing assets calculated as quick assets (cash, short-term investments, and receivables) divided by current liabilities.

10. An income statement account used to record cash shortages and cash overages arising from omitted petty cash receipts and from errors in making change.

11. Another name for acid-test ratio.

12. Lists the items such as currency, coins, and cheques deposited along with each of their dollar amounts.

13. Fundamental principles of internal control that apply to all companies requiring management to ensure transactions and activities are authorized, maintain records, insure assets, separate recordkeeping and custody of assets, establish a separation of duties, apply technological controls, and perform internal and external audits.

14. Cheques that the bank has paid and deducted from the customer's account during the month.

15. A characteristic of an asset that refers to how easily the asset can be converted into cash or another type of asset or used in paying for services or obligations.

16. An insurance policy purchased by a company to protect against losses from theft by that employee.

17. An act where two or more people agree to commit a fraud.

18. Includes the signatures of each person authorized to sign cheques from the account.

19. Those current assets that are most liquid, specifically cash, short-term investments, and receivables.

20. Includes currency, coins, and amounts on deposit in bank chequing or savings accounts.

21. An internal control principle requiring the division of responsibility for related transactions between two or more individuals or departments.

Problem IV

Complete the following by filling in the blanks.

1. If a cashier makes a mistake while making change and gives a customer too much money back, the resulting cash shortage is recorded with a debit to an account called
   _____.

2. Managers place a high priority on internal control systems to monitor and control operations because these systems can prevent_____, help managers _____, and monitor _____.

3. Maintaining adequate records helps protect _____ by ensuring that employees use _____.

4. If the size of the petty cash fund remains unchanged, the Petty Cash account _____ (is, is not) debited in the entry to replenish the petty cash fund.

5. Control of a small business is commonly gained through the direct supervision and active participation of the _____ in the affairs and activities of the business. However, as a business grows, it becomes necessary for the manager to delegate responsibilities and rely on _____ rather than personal contact in controlling the affairs and activities of the business.

6. A properly designed internal control system encourages adherence to prescribed managerial policies; and it also (a) _____
   _____;
   (b) _____
   _____; and (c) _____
   _____.

7. A good system of internal control for cash requires a _____ of duties so that the people responsible for handling cash and for its custody are not the same people who _____. It also requires that all cash receipts be deposited in the bank _____ and that all payments, except petty cash payments, be made by _____.

8. A bank reconciliation is prepared to account for the difference between the _____ and the _____.

9. A _____ of control requires that a number of procedures be performed and documents collected to support the validity of each disbursement.

10. A basic principle for controlling cash disbursements is that all payments are made by_____. An exception to this rule is made for _____.

11. To record the reimbursement of the petty cash fund, debit _____ and credit _____.

12. Good internal control follows certain broad principles. These principles are:

    (a) Establish responsibilities for each task clearly and to _____.

    (b) Maintain adequate records to help protect _____ by ensuring that employees use prescribed procedures.

    (c) _____ assets and _____ key employees.

    (d) Separate recordkeeping for assets and _____ of assets.

    (e) _____responsibility for related transactions.

    (f) Apply _____ controls such as time clocks or cash registers.

    (g) Perform regular and independent _____ to ensure internal control procedures are followed.

13. After preparing a bank reconciliation, journal entries _____(should, should not) be made to record those items listed as outstanding cheques.

14. The acid-test ratio, like the current ratio, divides _____ by _____ to measure a company's ability to cover current liabilities.

Problem V

On November 5 of the current year Cullen Company drew Cheque No. 23 for $50 to establish a petty cash fund.

1. Give the general journal entry to record the establishment of the fund.

DATE	ACCOUNT TITLES AND EXPLANATION	P.R.	DEBIT	CREDIT

After making a payment from petty cash on November 25, the petty cashier noted that there was only $2.50 cash remaining in the fund. The cashier prepared the following list of expenditures from the fund and requested that the fund be replenished.

Nov. 9   Express freight on merchandise purchased.................................... $ 9.75
  12   Miscellaneous expense to clean office............................... 10.00
  15   Office supplies 3.50
  18   Delivery of merchandise to customer 8.00
  23   Miscellaneous expense for faxes 3.25
  25   Express freight on merchandise purchased.................... 13.00

Cheque No. 97 in the amount of $47.50 was drawn to replenish the fund.

2. In the General Journal below give the entry to record the cheque replenishing the petty cash fund.

DATE	ACCOUNT TITLES AND EXPLANATION	P.R.	DEBIT	CREDIT

Problem VI

Information about the following eight items is available to prepare Noirot Company's December 31 bank reconciliation.

Two cheques (1) No. 453 and (2) No. 457 were outstanding on November 30. Cheque No. 457 was returned with the December bank statement but Cheque No. 453 was not. (3) Cheque No. 478, written on December 26, was not returned with the cancelled cheques; and (4) Cheque No. 480 for $96 was incorrectly entered in the Cash Disbursements Journal and posted as though it were for $69. (5) A deposit placed in the bank's night depository after banking hours on November 30 appeared on the December bank statement, but (6) one placed there after hours on December 31 did not. (7) Enclosed with the December bank statement was a debit memorandum for a bank service charge and (8) a cheque received from a customer and deposited on December 27 but returned by the bank marked "Not Sufficient Funds."

1. If an item in the above list should not appear on the December 31 bank reconciliation, ignore it. However, if an item should appear, enter its number in a set of parentheses to show where it should be added or subtracted in preparing the reconciliation.

NOIROT COMPANY
Bank Reconciliation
December 31, 2005

Book balance of cash	$X,XXX	Bank statement balance..................	$X,XXX
Add:		Add:	
( )		( )	
( )		( )	
( )		( )	
Deduct:		Deduct:	
( )		( )	
( )		( )	
( )		( )	
Reconciled balance	$X,XXX	Reconciled balance	$X,XXX

2. Certain of the above items require entries on Noirot Company's books. Place the numbers of these items within the following parentheses:

    (   ), (   ), (   ), (   ), (   ), (   )

Problem VII

The bank statement dated October 31, 2005, for Maui Company showed a balance of $2,426.25 which differs from the $1,658.25 book balance of cash on that date. In attempting to reconcile the difference, the accountant noted the following facts:

1. The bank recorded a service fee of $23 that was not recorded on the books of Maui Company.

2. A deposit of $1,236 was made on the last day of the month but was not recorded by the bank.

3. A cheque for $176 for office supplies had been recorded on the Maui Company books as $167. The bank paid the correct amount.

4. A cheque was written during October but has not been processed by the bank. The amount was $754.

5. A cheque for $973 is still outstanding from September.

6. A cheque from Aloha Company for $89 and deposited by Maui Company was returned marked "Not Sufficient Funds."

7. A credit memorandum stated that the bank collected a note receivable of $418 for Maui Company and charged Maui a $20 collection fee. Maui Company had not previously recorded the collection.

Prepare, in good form, a bank reconciliation which shows the correct cash balance on October 31, 2005. Prepare the journal entries resulting from the bank reconciliation.

Solutions for Chapter 9

Problem I

1. T   6. F
2. F   7. F
3. T   8. F
4. T
5. T

Problem II

1. C
2. C
3. C
4. B
5. D

Problem III

9	Acid-test ratio		8	Internal control system
1	Bank reconciliation		2	Liquid asset
16	Bond		15	Liquidity
14	Cancelled cheques		3	Petty cashier
20	Cash		13	Principles of internal control
10	Cash Over and Short account		11	Quick ratio
4	Cheque		19	Quick assets
17	Collusion		21	Separation of duties
7	Debit card		18	Signature card
12	Deposit slip		6	Voucher system
5	Electronic funds transfer			

Problem IV

1. Cash Over and Short

2. avoidable losses, plan operations, company and human performance

3. assets, prescribed procedures

4. is not

5. owner-manager, a system of internal control

6. (a) promotes efficient operations; (b) protects assets; and (c) ensures reliable accounting

7. separation, maintain the cash records, intact each day, cheque

8. book balance of cash, bank statement balance

9. voucher system

10. cheque, petty cash disbursements

11. various expense accounts, Cash

12. (a) one person; (b) assets; (c) insure, bond; (d) custody; (e) divide; (f) technological; (9) reviews

13. should not

14. quick assets, current liabilities

Problem V

1.	Nov. 5	Petty Cash	50.00	
		Cash		50.00
		Established a petty cash fund.		
2.	Nov. 25	Transportation-In	22.75	
		Miscellaneous Expenses	13.25	
		Office Supplies	3.50	
		Delivery Expense	8.00	
		Cash		47.50
		Reimbursed the petty cash fund.		

Problem VI

1. Book balance of cash .... $X,XXX   Bank statement balance .... $X,XXX
   Add: Add:
     (   )   (6)
   Deduct: Deduct:
     (4)   (1)
     (7)   (3)
     (8)   (   )

2.   (4), (7), (8)

Problem VII

MAUI COMPANY
Bank Reconciliation
October 31, 2005

Book balance of cash	$1,658.25	Bank statement balance..............	$2,426.25
Add:		Add:	
Proceeds of note less collection fee............	398.00	Deposit on October 31/05	1,236.00
	$2,056.25		$3,376.35
Deduct:		Deduct:	
NSF cheque ... $89.00		Outstanding cheques:	
Service fee....... 23.00		August $973.00	
Recording error 9.00	121.00	September 754.00	1,727.00
Reconciled balance	$1,935.25	Reconciled balance	$1,935.25

1. Oct.31	Cash		398.00	
	Collection Expense		20.00	
	Note Receivable			418.00
	Bank collection of note.			
2. Oct.31	Accounts Receivable – Aloha Company		89.00	
	Cash			89.00
	NSF cheque.			
3. Oct.31	Service Fee Expense		23.00	
	Cash			23.00
	Bank service fees.			
4. Oct.31	Office Supplies		9.00	
	Cash			9.00
	Correction of error.			

Learning Objective 1:

Describe accounts receivable and how they occur and are recorded.

Summary

Accounts receivable refer to amounts due from customers for credit sales. The subsidiary ledger lists the amounts owed by individual customers. Credit sales arise from at least two sources: (1) sales on credit and (2) credit card sales. Sales on credit refers to a company granting credit directly to customers. Credit card sales involve use of a third party issuing a credit card.

Learning Objective 2:

Apply the allowance method to account for accounts receivable.

Summary

Under the allowance method, bad debt expense is estimated at the end of the accounting period by debiting Bad Debt Expense and crediting the Allowance for Doubtful Accounts. When accounts are later identified as being uncollectible, they are written off by debiting the Allowance for Doubtful Accounts and crediting Accounts Receivable.

Learning Objective 3:

Estimate uncollectibles using approaches based on sales and accounts receivable.

Summary

Uncollectibles are estimated by focusing on either (a) the income statement relation between bad debt expense and credit sales or (b) the balance sheet relation between accounts receivable and the Allowance for Doubtful Accounts. The first approach emphasizes the matching principle for the income statement. The second approach can include either a simple percent relation with accounts receivable or the aging of accounts receivable. It emphasizes realizable value of accounts receivable for the balance sheet.

Learning Objective 4:

Apply the direct write-off method to account for uncollectible accounts receivable.

Summary

The direct write-off method debits Bad Debt Expense and credits Accounts Receivable when accounts are determined to be uncollectible. This method is acceptable only when the amount of bad debt expense is immaterial.

Learning Objective 5:

Describe a short-term note receivable and compute its maturity date and interest.

Summary

A note receivable is a written promise to pay a specified amount of money either on demand or at a definite future date, normally within the next 12 months or the business' operating cycle if greater than one year. The maturity date of a note is the day the note (principal and interest) must be repaid. Interest rates are typically stated in annual terms. When a note's time to maturity is more or less than one year, the amount of interest on a note is computed by expressing time as a fraction of one year and multiplying the note's principal by this fraction and the annual interest rate.

Learning Objective 6:

Record short-term notes receivable.

Summary

A note is recorded at its principal amount by debiting the Notes Receivable account. The credit amount is to the asset or service provided in return for the note. Interest is earned from holding a note. This interest is recorded for the time period it is held in the accounting period reported on. When a note is honoured, the payee debits the money received and credits both Notes Receivable and Interest Revenue. Dishonoured notes are credited to Notes Receivable and Interest Revenue and debited to Accounts Receivable.

Learning Objective 7 (Appendix 10A):

Explain how receivables can be converted to cash before maturity.

Summary

There are three usual means to convert receivables to cash before maturity. First, a company can sell accounts receivable to a factor, who charges a factoring fee. Second, a company can borrow money by signing a note payable that is secured by pledging the accounts receivable. Third, notes receivable can be discounted at a bank, with or without recourse. The full-disclosure principle requires companies to disclose the amount of receivables pledged and the contingent liability for notes discounted with recourse.

Learning Objective 8 (Appendix 10B):

Compute accounts receivable turnover and days' sales uncollected and use them to analyze liquidity.

Summary

Accounts receivable turnover and days' sales uncollected are measures of both the quality and liquidity of accounts receivable. The accounts receivable turnover measure indicates how often, on average, receivables are received and collected during the period and is computed as sales divided by average accounts receivable for the period. Days' sales uncollected is calculated as (accounts receivable divided by net sales) x 365 and is used to estimated how much time is likely to pass before cash receipts from net sales are received equal to the average amount of accounts receivable. Both ratios are compared to those for other companies in the same industry, and with prior years' estimates.

I.   **Accounts Receivable**—refers to an amount due from another party;
       also referred to as *trade receivables*.

   A. Recognizing *Accounts Receivable*: arise from credit sales to
      customers.

       1. Sales on credit: company must maintain a separate account
          receivable for each customer and account for bad debts from
          credit sales. At the time of the sale, debit Accounts
          Receivable and credit Sales for the full amount of the sale.

       2. Non-bank credit card:

          a. The retailer mails the credit card sales receipts and awaits
             payment. Debit Accounts Receivable and credit Sales for
             the full amount of the credit card sale. When cash is
             received, debit Cash for the amount received, debit Credit
             Card Expense and credit Accounts Receivable.

   B. Valuing Accounts Receivable—Two methods used to account for
      uncollectible accounts, or bad debts.

   C. Allowance Method—matches the expected loss from uncollectible
      accounts receivable against the sales they helped produce in that
      period.

       1. Recording estimated bad debt expense at the end of the
          accounting period—debit Bad Debt Expense, credit the
          contra-asset account called the *Allowance for Doubtful
          Accounts*.

       2. Method satisfies matching principle—expense is charged in
          period of related sale.

       3. Accounts Receivable are reported at their *realizable value*
          (A/Rec less the balance of the allowance account).

       4. Writing off a bad debt—debit Allowance for Doubtful
          Accounts, credit Accounts Receivable; does not change the
          estimated realizable value of Accounts Receivable.

       5. Recovery of a bad debt—debit Accounts Receivable and
          credit Allowance for Doubtful Accounts to reinstate the
          account; then debit Cash and credit Accounts Receivable to
          record the payment in full.

D. Estimating Bad Debt Expense—two methods:

1. *Percent of sales approach* (or *income statement approach*)—uses income statement relationships. Bad debt expense is calculated as a percentage of credit sales (or net sales).

2. *Accounts Receivable approach* (*balance sheet approach*)—uses balance sheet relationships. The required ending credit balance in Allowance for Doubtful Accounts is calculated as:

   a. Percent of accounts receivable—adjust Allowance for Doubtful Accounts (debit or credit) to achieve desired ending balance, and (credit or debit) Bad Debt Expense.

   b. *Aging of accounts receivable*, or *aging analysis*—same journal entry accounts.

E. Direct Write Off Method—records the loss from an uncollectible account receivable at the time it is determined to be uncollectible. No attempt is made to estimate uncollectible accounts or bad debt expense.

1. To write off an uncollectible: debit Bad Debt Expense, credit Accounts Receivable.

2. Conservatism—assets and net income must never be overstated; satisfied with the allowance method.

3. Matching principle—direct write-off method does not match revenues and expenses. Bad debt expense is not recorded until an account becomes uncollectible, often not occurring during the same account period.

II. **Short-Term Notes Receivable**—(*promissory note*) is a written promise to pay a specified amount of money either on demand or at a definite future date.

A. Maturity date—the date on which the principal is to be repaid, calculated as the date of the note plus the time period of the note (days, months or years).

C. Calculating interest:

$$\begin{matrix} \text{Principal of} \\ \text{note} \end{matrix} \times \begin{matrix} \text{Annual} \\ \text{rate of} \\ \text{interest} \end{matrix} \times \begin{matrix} \text{Time} \\ \text{expressed} \\ \text{in years} \end{matrix} = \text{Interest}$$

D. Receipt of a note—debit Notes Receivable for principal or face amount of note. Credit account will depends on reason note is received.

E. End-of-period interest adjustment—accrued interest is computed and recorded; debit Interest Receivable and credit Interest Revenue.

  F. Honouring a note—when the note is paid on its maturity date; debit Cash for maturity value (face + interest), credit Note Receivable for face amount and credit Interest Revenue (and possibly Interest Receivable) for the interest amount.

  G. Dishonouring a note—when a note is not paid on its maturity date, debit Accounts Receivable for maturity value (face + interest), credit Note Receivable for face amount and credit Interest Revenue for the interest amount.

III. **Converting Receivables to Cash before Maturity (Appendix 10A)**—reasons include the need for cash or a desire to not be involved in collection activities.

  A. Selling Accounts Receivable—buyer, called a *factor*, charges the seller a *factoring fee* and then collects the receivables as they come due.

  B. Pledging Accounts Receivable as Loan Security
   1. Borrower retains ownership of the receivables.
   2. If borrower defaults on the loan, the lender has the right to be paid from cash receipts as the accounts receivable are collected.
   3. The pledge should be disclosed in notes to financial statements.

  C. Discounting Notes Receivable—selling collection rights to bank or financial institution.
   1. With recourse—if the original maker of note fails to pay the bank when it matures, the original payee must pay.
    a. A company discounting a note has a *contingent liability* (an obligation to make a future payment if, and only if, an uncertain future event occurs) until the bank is paid.
   2. Without recourse—no contingent liability. Bank assumes the risk of a bad debt loss.

  D. Full-Disclosure—of contingent liabilities is required.

IV. **Using the Information (Appendix 10B)**

  A. *Accounts Receivable Turnover*
   1. Measure of liquidity; indicates how often receivables are received and collected during the period.
   2. Calculated as: $\dfrac{\text{Net sales}}{\text{Average accounts receivable}}$

  B. *Days' Sales Uncollected (Days' Sales in Receivables)*
   1. Estimates how much time is likely to pass before cash is received from credit sales equal to the current amount of accounts receivable.
   2. Calculated as: $\dfrac{\text{Average accounts receivable}}{\text{Net sales}} \times 365$

© *McGraw-Hill Ryerson, Inc., 2005*

Study Guide, Chapter 10   *10-187*

VISUAL #15
METHODS OF ACCOUNTING FOR BAD DEBTS

	DIRECT WRITE-OFF METHOD	ALLOWANCE METHOD
	Accounts for bad debts from an uncollectible account receivable at the time account is determined uncollectible.	At the end of each accounting period, bad debts expense is estimated and recorded.
Year end	No adjusting entry	Adjusting entry required: **Bad Debt Expense XXX** **Allowance for Uncollectible Accounts XXX** (The amount is an estimate based on a percent of sales or a percent of outstanding accounts receivable. If the estimate is based on sales, the full estimate is used in the adjusting entry. If the estimate is based on accounts receivable the allowance account balance is brought to the amount of the estimate.)
When an account is determined uncollectible.	Write-off entry required: **Bad Debts Expense XXX** **Accounts Receivable/Customer XXX** (The amount is the balance of the uncollectible account.)	Write-off entry required: **Allowance for Uncollectible Accounts XXX** **Accounts Receivable/Customer XXX** (The amount is the balance of the uncollectible account.)
When an account previously written off is recovered.	1. Reinstate account *by reversing write-off:* **Accounts Receivable/Customer XXX** **Bad Debts Expense XXX** (The amount is the account balance that was written off.) 2. Record collection on account normally: **Cash XXX** **Accounts Receivable/Customer XXX** (The amount is the amount collected.)	1. Reinstate account *by reversing write-off:* **Accounts Receivable/Customer XXX** **Allowance for Uncollectible Accounts XXX** (The amount is the account balance that was written off.) 2. Record collection on account normally: **Cash XXX** **Accounts Receivable/Customer XXX** (The amount is the amount collected.)
Advantages	• Does not require adjusting entry. • Does not require year-end estimating of uncollectibles.	• Matches expense against related revenues. • Reports the net realizable accounts receivable on the Balance Sheet (a more accurate reporting of assets).
Disadvantages	• Violates matching, therefore only allowed if qualified under materiality principle. (May be used by a business that anticipates an immaterial amount of uncollectibles.)	• Requires adjusting entry. • Requires year-end estimating of uncollectibles.

PROMISSORY NOTE

(1) April 15, 2005
    Date

(6) $2,000.00
    Amount

For value received, I promise to pay to the order of

(2) Plexi-Plus Supply Co.
    London, Ontario

(7) Two thousand and no/100 -------------------Dollars

(3) on   June 14, 2005

(4) plus interest at the annual rate of 9 percent.

(5) Scott Cooke
    for Tobay Sod Co.

Fundamental Accounting Principles, 11th Canadian Edition

Problem I

The following statements are either true or false. Place a (T) in the parentheses before each true statement and an (F) before each false statement.

1. ( ) Accounts receivable are also known as trade receivables.

2. ( ) If cash from credit card sales is received immediately when the credit card receipts are deposited at the bank, the credit card expense is recorded at the time the sale is recorded.

3. ( ) Businesses with credit customers need not maintain a separate account for each customer.

4. ( ) After all entries are posted, the sum of the balances in the Accounts Receivable Ledger should be equal to the balance of the Accounts Receivable account in the General Ledger.

5. ( ) Under the allowance method of accounting for bad debts, accounts receivable are reported on the balance sheet at the amount of cash proceeds expected from their collection.

6. ( ) Under the allowance method of accounting for bad debts, at the time an adjusting entry to record estimated bad debt expense is made, the debit side of the entry is to Accounts Receivable.

7. ( ) Under the allowance method of accounting for bad debts, when an account deemed uncollectible is written off against Allowance for Doubtful Accounts, the estimated realizable amount of Accounts Receivable is increased.

8. ( ) The journal entry to record recovery of a bad debt returns the amount paid to accounts receivable.

9. ( ) The income statement approach to estimating bad debts is based on the idea that some percentage of accounts receivable will be uncollectible.

10. ( ) The balance sheet approach to estimating bad debts is based on the idea that some particular percentage of accounts receivable will become uncollectible.

11. ( ) Aging of accounts receivable requires the examination of each account in the accounts receivable ledger.

12. ( ) The direct write-off method of accounting for bad debts records the loss from an uncollectible account receivable at the time it is determined to be uncollectible.

13. ( ) Although the direct write-off method of accounting for bad debts usually mismatches revenues and expenses, it may be allowed in cases where bad debt losses are immaterial in relation to total net sales and net income.

14. ( ) A promissory note is a unwritten promise the pay a specified amount of money either on demand or at a definite future date.

15. ( ) At maturity, the principal minus the interest owing on a note must be paid.

16. ( ) A 180-day note, dated May 5, matures on November 4 of the current year.

17. ( ) When notes receivable are outstanding at the end of an accounting period, accrued interest is computed and recorded only at the maturity date.

18. ( ) When a note receivable is discounted without recourse, the bank does not assume the risk of a bad debt loss.

19. ( ) When a note receivable is discounted with recourse, the company that discounts the note has a contingent liability.

20. ( ) A company that pledges its accounts receivable as security for a loan should disclose the fact in a note to the financial statements.

Problem II

You are given several words, phrases, or numbers to choose from in completing each of the following statements or in answering the following questions. In each case select the one that best completes the statement or answers the question and place its letter in the answer space provided.

_____ 1. Yellow Company uses the income statement method to calculate its bad debts, and the allowance to account for them. During the year, the credit Sales amounted to $240,000, and at the end of the year, outstanding accounts receivable amounted to $11,000. It was estimated that 4% of credit sales were uncollectible. What is the year-end adjusting journal entry to record bad debts?

a.	Accounts receivable	7,500.00	
	Allowance for doubtful accounts.......................		7,500.00
b.	Allowance for doubtful accounts	9,600.00	
	Bad debts expense		9,600.00
c.	Bad debts expense..	300.00	
	Cash		300.00
d.	Cash..	300.00	
	Bad debts expense		300.00
e.	Bad debts expense	9,600.00	
	Allowance for doubtful accounts.......................		9,600.00

_____ 2. Office Furniture Company uses the direct write-off method to calculate and account for bad debts. During the year, Sales amounted to $115,000, and at the end of the year, outstanding accounts receivable amounted to $4,500. Computing Company's account, for $400, was written off with the journal entry:

a.	Bad debts expense..	4,500.00	
	Allowance for doubtful accounts.......................		4,500.00
b.	Bad debts expense	400.00	
	Accounts receivable...		400.00
c.	Allowance for doubtful accounts	400.00	
	Accounts receivable...		400.00
d.	Accounts for doubtful accounts	4,500.00	
	Bad debts expense		4,500.00
e.	Accounts receivable	400.00	
	Bad debts expense		400.00

_____ 3. Jupiter Company has decided to write off the account of Jack Lewis against the Allowance for Doubtful Accounts. The $2,100 balance in Lewis' account originated with a credit sale in July of last year. What is the general journal entry to record this write-off?

a.	Allowance for Doubtful Accounts	2,100	
	Accounts Receivable—Jack Irwin.....................		2,100
b.	Accounts Receivable...	2,100	
	Allowance for Doubtful Accounts.....................		2,100
c.	Bad debt Expense...	2,100	
	Allowance for Doubtful Accounts.....................		2,100
d.	Accounts Receivable	2,100	
	Accounts Receivable—Jack Irwin.....................		2,100
e.	Bad Debt Expense	2,100	
	Accounts Receivable		2,100

_____ 4. Komatsu Corporation had credit sales of $4,000,000 in 2005. Before recording the December 31, 2005, adjustments, the company's Allowance for Doubtful Accounts had a credit balance of $2,800. A schedule of the December 31,2005, accounts receivable by age is summarized as follows:

December 31, 2005 Accounts Receivable	Age of Accounts Receivable	Uncollectible Percent Expected
$315,000	Not due	1.0
74,000	1–45 days past due	8.0
36,000	46–90 days past due	22.0
3,000	Over 90 days past due	80.0

Calculate the amount that should appear on the December 31, 2005, balance sheet as allowance for doubtful accounts.

a. $31,500
b. $3,150
c. $16,590
d. $22,190
e. $19,390

_____ 5. Based on the information given in problem 4, what is the general journal entry to record bad debt expense for 2005?

a. Debit Bad Debt Expense; credit Allowance for Doubtful Accounts.
b. Debit Accounts Receivable; credit Allowance for Doubtful Accounts.
c. Debit Bad Debt Expense; credit Accounts Receivable.
d. Debit Allowance for Doubtful Accounts; credit Bad Debt Expense.
e. Debit Accounts Receivable; credit Bad Debt Expense.

_____ 6. MBC Company discounts a $25,000 note receivable, with recourse, and receives proceeds of $25,250. MBC's entry to record the transaction would include the following:

a. $25,250 debit to Cash.
b. $250 debit to Interest Expense.
c. $250 debit to Loss on Sale of Notes.
d. $24,750 credit to Notes Receivable.
e. $25,000 credit to Notes Receivable and $250 credit to Interest Receivable.

_____ 7. Westing Company had net sales of $500,000 and $400,000 for 2006 and 2005, respectively. Accounts receivable at December 31, 2006 and 2005, were $45,000 and $55,000. What is Westing's accounts receivable turnover for 2006?

a. 11.1 times.
b. 10.0 times.
c. 20.0 times.
d. 9.0 times.
e. 7.3 times.

_____8. Alabaster Company had accounts receivable of $18,000 at the beginning of the year and $22,000 at the end. Net sales for the year amounted to $260,000. What is the company's days' sales uncollected?

    a. 30.9 days

    b. 28.1 days

    c. 25.3 days

    d. 14.4 days

    e. 13.0 days

Problem III

Many of the important ideas and concepts discussed in Chapter 10 are reflected in the following list of key terms. Test your understanding of these terms by matching the appropriate definitions with the terms. Record the number identifying the most appropriate definition in the blank space next to each term.

_____ Accounts receivable	_____ Factor
_____ Accounts receivable approach	_____ Honouring a note receivable
_____ Accounts receivable turnover	_____ Income statement approach
_____ Aging analysis	_____ Interest
_____ Aging of accounts receivable	_____ Maker of a note
_____ Allowance for Doubtful Accounts	_____ Maturity date of a note
_____ Allowance method of accounting for bad debts	_____ Non-bank credit card
_____ Bad debts	_____ Note receivable
_____ Balance sheet approach	_____ Payee of a note
_____ Contingent liability	_____ Percent of sales approach
_____ Creditor	_____ Percent of accounts receivable approach
_____ Date of a note	_____ Period of a note
_____ Days' sales uncollected	_____ Principal of a note
_____ Days' sales in receivables	_____ Promissory note
_____ Debtor	_____ Realizable value
_____ Direct write-off method	_____ Short-term note receivable
_____ Dishonouring a note receivable	_____ Trade receivables
_____ Due date of a note	_____ Uncollectible accounts

1. A card for which the retailer mails the credit card sales receipts and awaits payments from the credit-granting agency, which is not a bank.

2. The buyer of accounts receivable.

3. The date on which interest begins to accrue.

4. A promissory note that becomes due within the next 12 months or within the business's operating cycle if greater than 12 months.

5. A measure of both the quality and liquidity of accounts receivable; it indicates how often, on average, receivables are received and collected during the period; computed by dividing credit sales (or net sales) by the average accounts receivable balance.

6. A contra asset account with a balance equal to the estimated amount of accounts receivable that will be uncollectible.

7. The time from the date of the note to its maturity date or due date.

8. Another name for days' sales uncollected.

9. Another name for short-term note receivable.

10. The accounts of customers who do not pay what they have promised to pay; the amount is an expense of selling on credit.

11. Amounts due from customers for credit sales.

12. Another name for percent of sales approach.

13. An accounting procedure that (1) estimates and reports bad debt expense from credit sales during the period of the sales, and (2) reports accounts receivable as the amount of cash proceeds that are expected from their collection (their estimated realizable value).

14. When a note's maker is unable or refuses to pay at maturity.

15. One who signs a note and promises to pay it at maturity.

16. Another name for payee.

17. A written promise to pay a specified amount of money either on demand or at a definite future date.

18. Another name for aging of accounts receivable.

19. Uses income statement relations to estimate bad debts.

20. A method of accounting for bad debts that records the loss from an uncollectible account receivable at the time it is determined to be uncollectible; no attempt is made to estimate uncollectible accounts or bad debt expense.

21. Another name for accounts receivable approach.

22. An approach to estimating bad debts that assumes a percent of outstanding receivables is uncollectible.

23. A process of classifying accounts receivable in terms of how long they have been outstanding for the purpose of estimating the amount of uncollectible accounts.

24. Another name for maturity date.

25. An obligation to make a future payment if, and only if, an uncertain future event actually occurs.

26. The one to whom a promissory note is made payable.

27. A method of estimating bad debts using balance sheet relations.

28. When the maker of the note pays the note in full at maturity.

29. A measure of the liquidity of receivable computed by taking the average balance of receivables and dividing by the credit (or net) sales over the year just completed, and then multiplying by 365 (the number of days in a year).

30. Another name for bad debts.

31. The charge for using (not paying) money until a later date.

32. Another name for accounts receivable.

33. The amount that the signer of a promissory note agrees to pay back when it matures, not including the interest.

34. The expected proceeds from converting assets into cash.

35. The date on which a note and any interest are due and payable.

36. Another name for the maker of a note.

Problem IV

On March 15, Roberto Company received from Johnny Fellini, a customer, $200 in cash and a $800, 12%, 60-day note dated March 14 in granting a time extension on Fellini's past-due account. On March 31, Roberto Company recorded the accrued interest on the note, and Johnny Fellini paid the note and its interest on the following May 13. Complete the general journal entries to record these transactions.

DATE	ACCOUNT TITLES AND EXPLANATION	P.R.	DEBIT	CREDIT
March 15				
	Received cash and a note in granting a time extension			
	on a past-due account.			
March 31				
	To record accrued interest on a note receivable.			
May 14				
	Received payment of a note and interest.			

Problem V

On April 1 Roberto Company accepted a $1,500, 13%, 90-day note dated that day from a customer, Rosie Napoli, in granting a time extension on the customer's past-due account. When Roberto Company presented the note for payment on June 30, it was dishonoured, and on November 2 Roberto Company wrote off the debt as uncollectible. Present entries to record the dishonour and the write-off against the company's Allowance for Doubtful Accounts.

DATE	ACCOUNT TITLES AND EXPLANATION	P.R.	DEBIT	CREDIT
June 30				
	To charge the account of Rosie Napoli for her			
	dishonoured $1,500, 13%, 90-day note.			
November 2				
	To write off the uncollectible note of Rosie Napoli.			

Problem VI

On April 2 Roberto Company received from Julia Romero, a customer, a $1,000, 12%, 60-day note dated that day in granting a time extension on her past-due account. Roberto Company held the note until April 26 and then discounted it, with recourse, at its bank. The proceeds from discounting the note were $1,030.00. Complete the following

DATE	ACCOUNT TITLES AND EXPLANATION	P.R.	DEBIT	CREDIT
April 2				
	Received a note in granting a time extension on a			
	past-due account			
April 26				
	Discounted the Julia Romero note.			

Problem VII

Shea Company uses the allowance method in accounting for bad debt losses, and over the past several years it has experienced an average loss equal to one-half of 1% of its credit sales. During 2005 the company sold $1,750,000 of merchandise on credit, including a $238 credit sale to George Rousseau on March 5, 2005. The $238 had not been received by the year's end.

1. At the end of 2005 Shea Company, in providing for estimated bad debt losses, assumes history will repeat. As a result, it provides an allowance for 2005 estimated bad debts equal to _____ % of its $1,750,000 of 2005 credit sales; and the adjusting entry to record the allowance will appear as follows: (Complete the following entry.)

DATE	ACCOUNT TITLES AND EXPLANATION	P.R.	DEBIT	CREDIT
2005				
Dec. 31				
	To record estimated bad debts			

2. The debit of the foregoing entry is to the expense account, _____, which is closed to the _____ account at the end of the accounting period, just as any other expense account is closed.

3. The effect of the foregoing adjusting entry on the 2005 income statement of Shea Company is to cause an estimated amount of bad debt expense to be deducted from the $1,750,000 of revenue from 2005 charge sales. This complies with the accounting principle of _____ _____.

4. The credit of the foregoing adjusting entry is to the contra account _____ _____. On the December 31, 2005, balance sheet the balance of this contra account is subtracted from the balance of the _____ account to show the amount that is expected to be realized from the accounts receivable.

5. On March 31, 2006, the Accounts Receivable controlling account and the Allowance for Doubtful Accounts account of Shea Company had the following balances:

Accounts Receivable		Allowance for Doubtful Accounts	
Mar. 31 65,625			Mar. 31 4,475

A balance sheet which was prepared on March 31, 2006, would show that Shea Company expects to collect $ _____ of its accounts receivable.

6. On April 1, 2006, Shea Company decided the $238 account of George Rousseau (sale made on March 5 of the previous year) was uncollectible and wrote it off as a bad debt. (Complete the entry and post to the above T-accounts the portions affecting the accounts.)

DATE	ACCOUNT TITLES AND EXPLANATION	P.R.	DEBIT	CREDIT
2006				
Apr. 1				
	To write off the account of Gary Bellini			

7. If a balance sheet was prepared immediately after the entry writing off the uncollectible account of Gary Bellini was posted, it would show that Coastal Company expected to collect $ _____ of its accounts receivable. Consequently, the write-off _____ (did, did not) affect the net balance sheet amount of accounts receivable. Likewise, the entry writing off the account did not record an expense because the expense was anticipated and recorded in the _____ _____ entry made on December 31, 2005, the year of the sale.

Problem VIII

Pretzli Company sells almost exclusively for cash, but it does make a few small charge sales, and it also occasionally has a small bad debt loss which it accounts for by the direct write-off method.

1. Give below the entry made by Pretzli Company on February 5 to write off the $55 uncollectible account of Joan Bond (the goods were sold during the previous period.)

DATE	ACCOUNT TITLES AND EXPLANATION	P.R.	DEBIT	CREDIT
Feb. 5				

2. Writing off the foregoing bad debt directly to the Bad Debt Expense account violates the accounting principle of _____.
   However, due to the accounting principle _____
   the direct write-off is permissible in this case because the company's bad debt losses are very small in relation to its sales.

Problem IX

1. A company that ages its accounts receivable and increases its allowance for doubtful accounts to an amount sufficient to provide for estimated bad debts had a $75 debit balance in its Allowance for Doubtful Accounts account on December 31. If on that date it estimated that $1,800 of its accounts receivable were uncollectible, it should make a year-end adjusting entry crediting $ _____ to its Allowance for Doubtful Accounts account.

2. If the same company's Allowance for Doubtful Accounts account had a $155 credit balance on December 31, the year-end adjusting entry would credit $_____ to its Allowance for Doubtful Accounts.

Problem X

Windsor Company allows its customers to use two credit cards: the University National Bank credit card and the Community Credit Card. Using the information given below, prepare general journal entries for Windsor Company to record the following credit card transactions:

a) University National Bank charges a 3% service fee for sales on its credit card. As a commercial customer of the bank, Windsor Company receives immediate credit when it makes its daily deposit of sales receipts.

    May 2   Sold merchandise for $525 to customers who used the University National Bank credit card.

DATE	ACCOUNT TITLES AND EXPLANATION	P.R.	DEBIT	CREDIT

b) Community Credit Card Company charges 4% of sales for use of its card. Windsor Company submits accumulated sales receipts to Community Company and is paid within 30 days.

    May 3   Sold merchandise for $675 to customers using the Community Credit Card. Submitted receipts to Community Company for payment

       30   Received amount due from Community Credit Card Company.

DATE	ACCOUNT TITLES AND EXPLANATION	P.R.	DEBIT	CREDIT

Solutions for Chapter 10

Problem I

1. T	11. T
2. T	12. T
3. F	13. T
4. T	14. F
5. T	15. F
6. F	16. F
7. F	17. F
8. T	18. F
9. F	19. T
10. T	20. T

Problem II

1. E
2. B
3. A
4. E
5. A
6. C
7. B
8. B

Problem III

11	Accounts receivable	2	Factor
27	Accounts receivable approach	28	Honouring a note receivable
5	Accounts receivable turnover	12	Income statement approach
18	Aging analysis	31	Interest
23	Aging of accounts receivable	15	Maker of a note
6	Allowance for Doubtful Accounts	35	Maturity date of a note
13	Allowance method of accounting for bad debts	1	Non-bank credit card
10	Bad debts	9	Note receivable
21	Balance sheet approach	26	Payee of a note
25	Contingent liability	19	Percent of sales approach
16	Creditor	22	Percent of accounts receivable approach
3	Date of a note	7	Period of a note
29	Days' sales uncollected	33	Principal of a note
8	Days' sales in receivables	17	Promissory note
36	Debtor	34	Realizable value
20	Direct write-off method	4	Short-term note receivable
14	Dishonouring a note receivable	32	Trade receivables
24	Due date of a note	30	Uncollectible accounts

Problem IV

March 15	Cash	200.00	
	Notes Receivable	800.00	
	Accounts Receivable—Johnny Fellini		1,000.00
March 31	Interest Receivable ($800 × .12 × 17/365)	4.47	
	Interest Earned		4.47
May 14	Cash	815.78	
	Interest Receivable		4.47
	Interest Earned ($800 × .12 × 43/365)		11.31
	Notes Receivable		800.00

Problem V

June 30	Accounts Receivable—Rosie Napoli	1,548.08	
	Interest Earned...		48.08
	Notes Receivable		1,500.00
Dec. 20	Allowance for Doubtful Accounts	1,548.08	
	Accounts Receivable—Rosie Napoli		1,548.08

Problem VI

Apr. 2	Notes Receivable	1,000.00	
	Accounts Receivable—Julia Romero.............................		1,000.00
26	Cash	1,030.00	
	Notes Receivable		1,000.00
	Interest revenue..		30.00

Problem VII

1. One-half of 1%, or 0.5%

Dec. 31	Bad Debt Expense..	8,750.00	
	Allowance for Doubtful Accounts...............................		8,750.00

2. Bad Debt Expense, Income Summary
3. Matching revenues and expenses
4. Allowance for Doubtful Accounts, Accounts Receivable
5. $61,150
6.

Apr. 1	Allowance for Doubtful Accounts...	238.00	
	Accounts Receivable—George Rousseau		238.00

Accounts Receivable			Allowance for Doubtful Accounts		
Mar. 31 65,625				Mar. 31	4,475
	Apr. 1	238	Apr. 1	238	

7. $61,150, did not, adjusting.

Problem VIII

1.

Feb. 5	Bad Debt Expense..	55.00	
	Accounts Receivable—Joan Bond		55.00

2. Matching revenues and expenses, materiality

Problem IX

1. $1,875

2. $1,645

Problem X

a) May 2   Cash 509.25

Credit Card Expense ($525 × 0.03) 15.75

     Sales 525.00

b) May 3   Accounts Receivable—Community Company 675.00

     Sales.. 675.00

30   Cash 648.00

Credit Card Expense ($675 × 0.04) 27.00

     Accounts Receivable—Community Company 675.00

CHAPTER 11
PAYROLL LIABILITIES

Learning Objective 1:

List the taxes and other items frequently withheld from employees' wages.

Summary

Amounts withheld from employees' wages include federal income taxes, Canada (or Quebec) Pension Plan (CPP or QPP) and employment insurance (EI). Payroll costs levied on employers include EI and CPP (or QPP). An employee's gross pay may be the employee's specified wage rate multiplied by the total hours worked plus an overtime premium rate multiplied by the number of overtime hours worked. Alternatively, it may be the given periodic salary of the employee. Taxes withheld and other deductions for items such as union dues, insurance premiums, and charitable contributions are subtracted from gross pay to determine the net pay.

Learning Objective 2:

Make the calculations necessary to prepare a Payroll Register and prepare the entry to record and pay payroll.

Summary

A Payroll Register is used to summarize all employees' hours worked, regular and overtime pay, payroll deductions, net pay, and distribution of gross pay to expense accounts during each pay period. It provides the necessary information for journal entries to record the accrued payroll and to pay the employees.

Learning Objective 3:

Calculate the payroll costs levied on employers and prepare the entries to record the accrual and payment of these amounts.

Summary

When a payroll is accrued at the end of each pay period, payroll deductions and levies also should be accrued with debits and credits to the appropriate expense and liability accounts.

Learning Objective 4:

Calculate and record employee fringe benefit costs and show the effect of these items on the total cost of employing labour.

Summary

Fringe benefit costs that involve simple cash payments by the employer should be accrued with an entry similar to the one used to accrue payroll levies. Legislated employee benefits related to Workers' Compensation and vacation pay are paid for by the employer.

Chapter Outline

I.   Payroll Accounting

A. Records cash payments to employees.

B. Provides valuable information regarding labour costs.

C. Accounts for amounts withheld from employees' pay.

D. Accounts for employee (fringe) benefits and payroll costs paid by the employer.

E. Provides the means to comply with governmental regulations on employee compensation.

II.   Items Withheld from Employees' Wages

A. Employee's income tax

1. Employers are required to calculate, collect, and remit to the Receiver General for Canada the income taxes of their employees.

2. The amount withheld is determined by wages and amount of *personal tax credits*.

3. Employers withhold income tax owed by each employee every payday based on an employee's completed Personal Tax Credit Return, Form TD1.

4. Payroll deduction tables are provided by the *Canada Customs and Revenue Agency (CCRA)*.

B. Canada (or Quebec) Pension Plan (CPP or QPP)—for working people between ages 18 and 70. The employer's contribution matches the employee's deduction.

C. Employment Insurance (EI)—for employed people. The employer's contribution equals 1.4 times the amount of the employee's deduction. The employer must complete a "Record of Employment" when employment is terminated.

D. T-4 forms—a year-end statement completed by the employer showing wages and deductions for the year; must be given to each employee on or before the last day of February of the following year.

E. Wages, Hours and Union Contracts—maximum hours of work and minimum pay rates are established by each province; with union contracts, the employer deducts dues from the wages of each employee and remits the amounts deducted to the union.

F. Other deductions—authorized individually by each employee: Canada Savings Bonds, health, accident, hospital or life insurance premiums, loan repayment, payment for merchandise purchased, donations to charitable organizations.

III. **The Payroll Register**

A. Payroll register—summarizes the total hours worked for each employee for a pay period.

B. The regular pay plus overtime premium pay is the *employee's gross pay.*

C. An employees' gross pay less total deductions is the *employee's net pay.*

D. Recording the payroll—general journal entry: debits to expense accounts and credits to various payable accounts.

E. Paying the employees: businesses pay employees by:

 1. Cheque, or

 2. Electronic funds transfer (EFT).

E. Employee's Individual Earnings Record—provides for each employee, in one record, a full year's summary of the employee's working time, gross earnings, deductions, and net pay. The information is taken from the Payroll Register; supplies data for the T4 slip.

IV. **Payroll Deductions Required of the Employer**

A. Canada Pension Plan—the employer must pay an amount equal to the sum of the employees' CPP (or QPP); debit CPP (or QPP) expense and credit CPP (or QPP) payable.

B. Employment Insurance—the employer is required to pay EI that is 1.4 times the sum of the employees' EI deductions; debit EI expense and credit EI payable.

C. Paying the payroll deductions—payables recorded as current liabilities until paid to the Receiver General for Canada; payment is usually required before the 15th of the month following; debit EI payable, debit Employees' income taxes payable, debit CPP (or QPP) payable, and credit Cash.

D. Remit other deductions—debit individual payable and credit Cash.

V. **Employee (Fringe) Benefit Costs**

A. *Employee fringe benefits*—benefits paid by companies in addition to wages earned; may include payment for medical insurance, life insurance, and disability insurance, contributions to a retirement income plan.

B. Workers' Compensation—provincial legislation requires employer to insure their employees against injury or disability that may arise as a result of employment.

Chapter Outline

C. Insurance and retirement plans—employers may pay insurance premiums or make contributions to retirement funds for the employees.

D. Vacation Pay—employers are required to allow their employees paid vacation time at a minimum rate of 4% of gross earnings: two weeks' vacation in return for working 50 weeks each year; employer should record estimated vacation pay with a debit to Benefits expense and a credit to Estimated vacation pay liability. The vacation time taken, with pay from the liability, is subject to the mandatory payroll deductions and employee benefits costs.

Problem I

The following statements are either true or false. Place a (T) in the parentheses before each true statement and an (F) before each false statement.

1. (   ) According to law, a T-4 form showing wages earned and taxes withheld must be given to each employee within two months after the year-end.

2. (   ) Employment insurance is withheld from employees' wages at the rate of 2.4% (2003).

3. (   ) Canada Pension Plan amounts are levied equally on the employee and the employer.

4. (   ) Employee (fringe) benefit costs represent expenses to the employer in addition to the direct costs of salaries and wages.

5. (   ) Each time a payroll is recorded, a general journal entry should also be made to record the employer's employment insurance cost.

6. (   ) Since income taxes withheld from an employee's wages are expenses of the employee, not the employer, they should not be treated as liabilities of the employer.

7. (   ) Since Jacques Company has very few employee accidents, the company has received a very favourable Workers' Compensation rating. As a result, Jacques Company should expect to pay smaller amounts of Worker's Compensation premium than normal.

Problem II

You are given several words, phrases or numbers to choose from in completing each of the following statements or in answering the following questions. In each case select the one that best completes the statement or answers the question and place its letter in the answer space provided

Use the following information as to earning and deductions for the pay period ended November 15 taken from a company's payroll records for the next two questions:

Employee's Name	Earnings to End of Previous Week	Gross Pay This Week	Income Tax	Medical Insurance Deducted
Jennifer Hawkins	$25,700	$ 600	$135.00	$ 35.50
Tyler Braun	20,930	700	144.00	35.50
Jason Lee	49,900	1,000	193.00	42.00
Kosta Paulus	18,400	800	132.00	42.00
		$3,100	$604.00	$155.00

_____ 1. Employees' EI and CPP are withheld at an assumed 7% rate on the first $39,000 paid each employee. A general journal entry to accrue the payroll should include a:

a. Debit to Accrued Payroll Payable for $3,100.
b. Debit to EI and CPP Payable for $205.80.
c. Debit to Payroll Expense for $147.00.
d. Credit to EI and CPP Payable for $147.00.
e. Credit to Accrued Payroll Payable for $2,194.00.

_____ 2. Assume that Canada Pension Plan applies at a rate of 4.95% on the $36,400 of eligible earnings. The general journal entry to record the employer's payroll cost resulting from the payroll should include a debit to Salaries Expense for:

a. $34.65
b. $103.95
c. $145.53
d. $153.45
e. The entry should be a credit to Payroll Expense.

_____ 3. In addition to determining and withholding income tax from each employee's wages, employers are required to:

    a. periodically deposit the withheld taxes with Canada Customs and Revenue Agency.

    b. file a quarterly report showing the income taxes withheld.

    c. give each employee a Wage and Tax Statement for the year, Form T-4.

    d. send Canada Customs and Revenue Agency copies of all T-4 forms given employees.

    e. All of the above.

Problem III

Many of the important ideas and concepts that are discussed in Chapter 11 are reflected in the following list of key terms. Test your understanding of these terms by matching the appropriate definitions with the terms. Record the number identifying the most appropriate definition in the blank space next to each term.

_____ Canada Pension Plan	_____ Employee's net pay
_____ Employee fringe benefits	_____ Payroll deductions
_____ Employment insurance	_____ Personal tax credits
_____ Employee's gross pay	_____ Wage bracket withholding table
_____ Employee's Individual Earnings Record	

1. Amounts deducted from an employee's pay, usually based on the amount of an employee's gross pay.

2. The amount an employee earns before any deductions for taxes or other items such as union dues or insurance premiums.

3. A national contributory retirement pension scheme.

4. A record of an employee's hours worked, gross pay, deductions, net pay, and certain personal information about the employee.

5. Amounts that may be deducted from an individuals' income taxes and that determine the amount of income taxes to be withheld.

6. A table showing the amounts to be withheld from employees' wages at various levels of earnings.

7. Payments by an employer, in addition to wages and salaries, that are made to acquire employee benefits such as insurance coverage and retirement income.

8. The amount an employee is paid, determined by subtracting from gross pay all deductions for taxes and other items that are withheld from the employee's earnings.

9. An employment/employer-financed unemployment insurance plan.

Problem IV

Complete the following by filling in the blanks.

1. An employee who works 45 hours in one week must normally be paid his or her regular rate of pay for the 45 hours plus overtime premium pay at one-half his or her regular rate for _____ of the 45 hours.

2. Funds for the payment of federal retirement benefits are raised by payroll deductions imposed under a law called the

   _____.

3. The amount to be withheld from an employee's wages for federal income taxes is determined by
   (a)_____

   and (b)_____.

4. Weekly employment benefits received by workers are based on _____

   _____prior to employment ceasing.

5. The Canada Pension Plan Act levies a payroll tax on both covered employers and their employees. In 2003, an employer was required to withhold CPP deductions from the wages of employees at the rate of _____% of each employee's gross earnings in excess of the allowed exemption, the withholding to continue each year until the contribution exempt point is reached. In addition to the employee's CPP withholdings, an employer must also pay a CPP amount equal to the sum of the _____ withheld from the wages of all of its employees.

6. The computation of income tax withholding deductions is facilitated by the use of _____

   _____ provided by Canada Customs and Revenue Agency.

7. Employers are required to remit the payroll deductions and withheld income taxes to the _____
   _____ on or before the
   _____ following that in which withholdings were made.

8. On or before the last day of _____following each year, an employer must give each employee a _____. A summary of information contained in the _____ supported by copies of statements issued to the employees is forwarded to the _____
   .

9. Worker's compensation premiums are paid in total by the _____and are normally based on
   (a)_____and   (b)
   _____.

Problem V

The Payroll Register of Brightlights Sales for the second week of the year follows. It has the deductions and net pay of the first three employees calculated and entered.

1. Mr. Yancy's deductions are as follows:

Canada Pension Plan	$35.33
Employment Insurance	29.81
Income Taxes	220.80
Medical Insurance	25.00

		DAILY TIME											EARNINGS			
EMPLOYEE'S NAME	CLOCK CARD NUMBER	M	T	W	T	F	S	S	TOTAL HOURS	O.T. HOURS	REG. PAY RATE	REGULAR PAY	O.T. PREMIUM PAY	GROSS PAY	
Rowena Brown	11	8	8	8	7	4	0	0	35		18 00	630 00		630 00	1
Ivor Sabatsky	8	8	8	8	5	4	0	0	33		20 00	660 00		660 00	2
Eva Queue	14	8	8	7	8	4	0	0	35		22 00	770 00		770 00	3
Fred Rasmussen	5	8	8	8	8	8	4	0	44	4	24 00				4
															5

Week ending January 14, 2005

	DEDUCTIONS					PAYMENT		DISTRIBUTION		
	EI	CPP	INCOME TAXES	MEDICAL INSURANCE	TOTAL DEDUC- TIONS	NET PAY	CHEQUE NUMBER	SALES SALARIES	OFFICE SALARIES	SHOP SALARIES
1	17 01	20 16	126 00	30 00	193 17	436 83		630 00		
2	17 82	21 12	132 00	28 00	198 94	461 06				660 00
3	20 79	24 64	154 00	25 00	224 43	545 57				770 00
4										
5										

2. Complete the Payroll Register by totalling its columns, and give the general journal entry to record its information.

DATE	ACCOUNT TITLES AND EXPLANATION	P.R.	DEBIT	CREDIT

3. In the space below give the general journal entry to record the payroll taxes levied on Brightlights as a result of the payroll entered in its January 14 Payroll Register.

DATE	ACCOUNT TITLES AND EXPLANATION	P.R.	DEBIT	CREDIT

4. On the next page is the individual earnings record of Fred Rasmussen. Transfer from the Payroll Register to Mr. Rasmussen's earnings record the payroll data for the second pay period of the year.

EMPLOYEE'S INDIVIDUAL EARNINGS RECORD

EMPLOYEE'S NAME	Fred Rasmussen
	S.I. ACCT. NO. 119-051-879
	EMPLOYEE NO. 5
HOME ADDRESS	2590 Columbia Street
NOTIFY IN CASE OF EMERGENCY	Karen Rasmussen
PHONE NUMBER	965-5698
EMPLOYED	1/9/98
DATE OF TERMINATION	
REASON	
DATE OF BIRTH	May 20, 1968
BECOMES 65	May 20, 2033
MALE (X) FEMALE ( )	MARRIED (X) SINGLE ( )
NUMBER OF DEPENDENTS 4	
PAY RATE $24.00	
OCCUPATION	Manager PLACE Store and Office

DATE		TIME LOST		TIME WK.													
PER. ENDS	PAID	HRS.	REASON	TOTAL	O.T. HOURS	REG. PAY	O.T. PREM. PAY	GROSS PAY	CPP	EI	INCOME TAXES	MEDICAL INSUR-ANCE	TOTAL DEDUC-TIONS	NET PAY	CHEQUE NUMBER	CUMU-LATIVE PAY
Jan. 7	Jan. 10	8	NY	32	0	768 00		768 00	24 58	20 74	153 60	25 00	223 92	544 08	095	768 00

McGraw-Hill Ryerson, Inc., 2005

11-213

Fundamental Accounting Principles, 11th Canadian Edition

Solutions for Chapter 11

Problem I

1. T   5. T
2. F   6. F
3. T   7. T
4. T

Problem II

1. D
2. B
3. E

Problem III

3	Canada Pension Plan	8	Employee's net pay
7	Employee fringe benefits	1	Payroll deductions
9	Employment insurance	5	Personal tax credits
2	Employee's gross pay	6	Wage bracket withholding table
4	Employee's Individual Earnings Record		

Problem IV

1. five

2. Canada Pension Plan

3. (a) the amount of his or her wages,

   (b) the number of his or her exemptions.

4. the average weekly wages.

5. 4.95%; amounts

6. tax withholding tables

7. Receiver General for Canada; 15th of the month

8. February; T-4 statement; T-4 statements; District Taxation Office.

9. employer (a) accident experience of the industrial classification of the business;

   (b) the total payroll.

Problem V

1., 2., & 3.

EMPLOYEE'S NAME	CLOCK CARD NUMBER	M	T	W	T	F	S	S	TOTAL HOURS	O.T. HOURS	REG. PAY RATE		REGULAR PAY		O.T. PREMIUM PAY		GROSS PAY		
Rowena Brown	11	8	8	8	7	4	0	0	35		18	00	630	00	0	00	630	00	1
Ivor Sabatsky	8	8	8	8	5	4	0	0	33		20	00	660	00	0	00	660	00	2
Eva Queue	14	8	8	7	8	4	0	0	35		22	00	770	00	0	00	770	00	3
Fred Rasmussen	5	8	8	8	8	8	4	0	44	4	24	00	1056	00	48	00	1104	00	4
													3116	00	48	00	3164	00	5

Week ending January 14, 2005

	EI			CPP			INCOME TAX			MEDICAL INSURANCE			TOTAL DEDUC-TIONS			NET PAY			CHEQUE NUMBER	SALES SALARIES			OFFICE SALARIES			SHOP SALARIES		
1	17	01		20	16		126	00		30	00	193	17		436	83		102	630	00									
2	17	82		21	12		132	00		28	00	198	94		461	06		103							660	00	
3	20	79		24	64		154	00		25	00	224	43		545	57		104							770	00	
4	29	81		35	33		220	80		25	00	310	94		793	06		105			1104	00					
5	85	43	1	01	25		632	80	1	08	00	927	48	2	236	52			630	00	1104	00	1	430	00	

1.	Jan. 7	Sales Salaries Expense..	630.00	
		Office Salaries Expense...	1,104.00	
		Shop Salaries Expense..	1,430.00	
		Canada Pension Plan Payable..		101.25
		Employment Insurance Payable...		85.43
		Employees' Income Taxes Payable		632.80
		Medical Insurance Payable..		108.00
		Accrued Payroll Payable..		2,236.52
3.	Jan. 7	Payroll Taxes Expense..	220.85	
		Canada Pension Plan Payable..		101.25
		Employment Insurance Payable...		119.60

EMPLOYEE'S INDIVIDUAL EARNINGS RECORD

EMPLOYEE'S NAME ___ Fred Rasmussen ___

S.I. ACCT. NO. ___ 119-051-879 ___   EMPLOYEE NO. ___ 5 ___

HOME ADDRESS ___ 2590 Columbia Street ___

NOTIFY IN CASE OF EMERGENCY ___ Karen Rasmussen ___

PHONE NUMBER ___ 965-5698 ___

EMPLOYED ___ 1/9/98 ___   DATE OF TERMINATION _____   REASON _____

DATE OF BIRTH ___ May 20, 1968 ___   DATE BECOMES 65 ___ May 20, 2033 ___

MALE (X)   FEMALE ( )

MARRIED (X)   SINGLE ( )

NUMBER OF DEPENDENTS ___ 4 ___

PAY RATE ___ $24.00 ___

OCCUPATION ___ Manager ___   PLACE ___ Store and office ___

| DATE | | TIME LOST | | TIME WK. | | | | | | | | | | | | |
PER. ENDS	PAID	HRS.	REASON	TOTAL	O.T. HOURS	REG. PAY	O.T. PREM. PAY	GROSS PAY	CPP	EI	INCOME TAXES	MEDICAL INSUR-ANCE	TOTAL DEDUC-TIONS	NET PAY	CHEQUE NUMBER	CUMU-LATIVE PAY
Jan. 7	Jan. 10	8	NY	32	0	768 00		768 00	24 58	20 74	153 60	25 00	223 92	544 08	095	768 00
14	16			44	4	1056 00	48 00	1104 00	35 33	29 81	220 80	25 00	310 94	793 06	105	1872 00